DANIEL

BEING FAITHFUL IN UNCERTAIN TIMES

MICHAEL T. GOWEN

malcolm down
PUBLISHING

First published 2023 by Malcolm Down Publishing Ltd.
www.malcolmdown.co.uk

25 24 23 22 7 6 5 4 3 2 1

British Library Cataloguing in Publication Data
A catalogue record for this book is available from the British Library.

ISBN 978-1-915046-35-2

Cover design by Esther Kotecha
Art direction by Sarah Grace

Printed in the UK

Endorsements

From Michael Gowen's book

Daniel: Being Distinctive in Uncertain Times

A well-written, deeply researched, and thoughtful reflection on living in uncertain and challenging times. There is a great deal of helpful food for thought here as we seek to be faithful to Christ in today's society.

Paul Harcourt, National Leader, New Wine

When I was in Sunday school we used to sing a chorus called 'Dare to Be a Daniel' and that's exactly what this book challenges us to do. Michael Gowen introduces us to the remarkable, yet in some respects very ordinary character of Daniel, drawing practical lessons for Christians of all ages and from all strata of society. Highly recommended for all who want to live an authentic Christian life in the challenging twenty-first century.

Mervyn Thomas CMG, Founder President of CSW

I'm so delighted to see this book in publication. The experience and wisdom that Michael has gleaned over decades will inspire and inform anyone who is inquisitive and committed to thriving in life, work and faith. You'll find a thoughtful blend of excellent biblical insights, faithfully understood in their historical context, alongside cultural commentary and space for personal reflection. An excellent devotional.

Andrew McNeil, Senior Pastor of Birmingham Vineyard and Associate National Director of Vineyard Churches UK and Ireland

Our world is in crisis. Plagues, fires, environmental calamity, nations are being shaken. Leaders are falling and rising. This book is a vivid reminder that the Lord God Almighty is devoted to his people and his Church. Michael graphically points out the timeless truth that God has the ability to both save and protect his beloved. The book of Daniel is a treasure chest of wisdom and provocation for any student of the Word. Michael is doing a great service to today's Church by taking us gently by the hand and guiding us chapter by chapter to true truth. A book that will build resilience and strength into every thinking Christian.

Eddie Lyle, President, Open Doors UK and Ireland

Perhaps you do not think of yourself as a radical evangelist whose ministry will help fundamentally change society? In this book Michael Gowen explains how Daniel found himself in a very similar situation, and draws practical wisdom from Daniel's experience which may prove helpful to those who are willing to make a difference for the kingdom of Jesus in the workplace environment. Warmly recommended!

Menno Helmus, National Director for the Association of Vineyard Churches in the Benelux

Michael shows us how Daniel's journey is one of human survival and resilience. No matter how far one falls or things go pear-shaped, God is still in the business of redemption. This is a story of the grace and faithfulness of God and that his Word is integral. It's an introspective journey into our relationship with God and a reminder that we can seek and depend on the grace of God in our day-to-day ordinary lives. I thoroughly enjoyed the read. It's an absolute blockbuster!

Bishop Arnold Muwonge, Founder and CEO, NDE-Network

For my three children and seven grandchildren
'Children are a heritage from the LORD'
(Psalm 127:3)

I thank him for the wonderful heritage that he has given me.

I thank him too for enabling me to experience
the blessing of Psalm 128:6:
'May you live to see your children's children'

Contents

INTRODUCTION

This book shows how chapters 4-6 of the book of Daniel in the Bible, although they were written two and a half millennia ago, are highly relevant to life today. It examines the issue of faithfulness through the lens of Daniel's life in middle and old age. He was able to stay faithful to God and faithful to the kings he served right to the end of his life, despite the many difficult moral choices, challenges and threats that he faced along the way.

This book also taps into issues of faithfulness in society today. In years gone by, my faithfulness, say, to a particular bank would be rewarded by being valued as an esteemed customer and being personally known by my local branch manager. Now we are rewarded for being unfaithful, for regularly switching to another bank, another energy provider or another insurer.

Both my father and my father-in-law worked for the same company all their working lives, and the company acted faithfully towards them. Now it is not unusual to have had half a dozen jobs before the age of forty; and many companies have no compunction in making long-serving staff redundant when it suits them.

In personal relationships, questions are being asked whether it is any longer necessary to remain faithful to the same person in marriage for a whole lifetime. Is it not preferable to accept when a marriage is dead and move on to another partner? Should we not have more 'open' marriages, where we avoid the boredom of one partner and relate sexually to other people as well?

Christians, as much as anybody else, face these important moral questions in today's society. However, they rely not just on the debate going on in society, but also on the book that guides them in the conduct of their life, the Bible. That book says that faithfulness is an important characteristic to value because it is one of the fruits of the Holy Spirit (see Galatians 5:22).

When the life of God enters into our inner being, through his Spirit, faithfulness will inevitably develop. This is also a reflection of the man whom we are called to follow. His name 'is called Faithful and True' (Revelation 19:11). As the life of God works within us, we are called to reproduce Jesus' character in our lives. Daniel will help us to understand how we can cooperate with God in this process.

My first book, *Daniel: Being Distinctive in Uncertain Times*,[1] covered the earlier period of his life in Daniel, chapters 1-3. However, you do not have to have read that book, because the only links between it and this present book are that they both cover parts of the book of Daniel, they are written by the same author, and they have the same basic format.

Like my first book, this is a devotional volume. But it does not set out to guide your daily Bible study over a defined period of time. What I have sought to do is to let you in on my conversations with God as I have worked through these three chapters of the book of Daniel, and to encourage you to reflect on the issues which are raised. Through this, I hope that you might be stimulated to engage with God yourself through reading the Bible.

I feel passionately about engaging with God through reading the Bible, because it has been one of the bedrocks of my own Christian faith

1. Malcolm Down Publishing, 2021.

over the past fifty years. I seek to begin each day by reading the Bible and asking God to communicate with me through it. Some days it is quite hard work; other days it flows freely. The more I do it, the easier it becomes. I would say that this daily habit of devotional Bible reading is the one thing more than any other that has kept me close to God and has enabled me to develop a deeper intimacy with him.

I was encouraged to learn from the pastoral and mission leader Dr David P. Teague that my experience is far from unique. He recounts:

> Once I asked several hundred people in a survey the following questions: (1) 'How much do you read the Bible?' and (2) 'How close do you feel toward God?' In the survey, the more that people read the Bible, the closer they said they felt to God. The relationship proved linear: any increase in Bible reading was associated with a closer feeling to God.[2]

As in my own daily Bible study, I have carefully and prayerfully read each passage in Daniel 4-6. I have written down what has come out of my conversations with God, focusing particularly on the application of these chapters to the world that we live in today. So, this is not a theological commentary with a comprehensive verse-by-verse exposition of the text. Nor does it give detailed analyses of the structure of the text. Nor does it quote and compare the work of other commentators.

I have divided the book into bite-sized portions. At the end of each section there are reflection questions, written in the first person, so that they are personal for you. Each section stands alone, but they flow with the Bible text. At times I have paused to develop over one or more

2. Dr David P. Teague with Dr Harvey Shepard, *Godly Leadership* (Bayswater, Victoria: Grassroots Mission Publications, Interserve, 2010), p. 45.

sections an important theme which is highlighted in the passage that we are reading. A suggestion as to how you might use this book is given in Appendix A at the back of the book.

I have chosen to write about Daniel because he is one of my Bible heroes. For the forty years of my working life I was employed in organisations that had no faith basis. For twenty-five of those years I was part of a large international governmental organisation, a kind of modern-day equivalent of the multi-cultural, multi-lingual court of the Babylonian Empire where Daniel worked. So, the fact that he remained faithful to God, often in very challenging circumstances, has been an inspiration to me.

This book was finalised in the second quarter of 2022, when the uncertainties and fears created by the Covid-19 pandemic were still being worked through by many people, and when those fears and uncertainties were being compounded by Russia's invasion of Ukraine and the explosion in energy prices and the inflation which it has brought in its wake.

The book of Daniel gives us many insights into what is happening in the world today and pointers as to how the future might develop; but this book makes no claim to any detailed predictions of how the present situation might be resolved, nor of any other future events.

Websites which are referred to were most recently accessed in the second quarter of 2022.

As we unpack this book together and with God, my prayer is that you will find that Daniel's life is speaking into your life, as it has into mine. The Bible tells us that Abel, the second human being to be born on earth, is still speaking today through his faith (see Hebrews 11:4). Daniel lived a long while after Abel, and through his faith he too is still speaking. His context and culture were radically different from yours and mine. Technology has advanced in ways that he could not even have dreamt of. But human nature has not significantly changed in the two and a half millennia since he was on the earth.

The Bible testifies that 'the word of God', given by revelation to the human race, 'is alive and active. Sharper than any double-edged sword, it penetrates even to dividing soul and spirit, joints and marrow; it judges the thoughts and attitudes of the heart' (Hebrews 4:12). This is true of the book of Daniel as much as any of the other sixty-five books of the Bible.

That living, active Word, when applied to our everyday lives, brings us into a deeper level of relationship with God. 'All Scripture is God-breathed' (2 Timothy 3:16). When we open our hearts and minds and study the Bible expectantly, we enter into contact with the very breath of God. We are able to experience the transforming power of his Holy Spirit, so that we can become channels of his life in our everyday situations. That has been my experience as I have studied the book of Daniel. I pray that it may be yours too.

About Michael Gowen

I was born in Northamptonshire and spent my teenage years in Leicester, both in the English East Midlands. My parents took me every Sunday to the local Anglican church, but I found little evidence of authentic spiritual life there. When Jesus Christ broke into my life at the age of eighteen and I decided to follow him, I discovered that, despite my church upbringing, I knew very little of the Bible. It seemed such a large, daunting book. So, I started opening it at random and reading whatever was before me. The more I read, the more I wanted to read; and I have continued reading the Bible for the past fifty years.

I am married, with three grown-up children and seven grandchildren, who are all wonderful (of course!). My wife of forty-eight years, Liz, has been a teacher and a psychotherapist, and is now a Spiritual Director.

She has constantly inspired, encouraged and challenged me. She is my No. 1 Fan and my No. 1 Critic. I could not wish for a better life partner.

I graduated in mathematics from the University of Manchester. I have worked variously as a probation officer (a kind of court social worker); promoting the interests of the deep sea and inshore fishing industries in Yorkshire and East Anglia; and for a large inter-governmental organisation in Brussels, Belgium, at one time or another in the areas of energy conservation, international trade agreements and humanitarian aid.

Throughout our married life, Liz and I have been involved bi-vocationally in church leadership: in free evangelical, Anglican and Vineyard churches. Nine years ago, I took early retirement from my job, and we came to live in the West Midlands in the UK, where we have been very well received in Birmingham Vineyard Church. We are involved in training, mentoring and encouraging leaders, and I regularly visit countries in Latin America and Africa (when Covid restrictions permit) to encourage Christians there.

To contact me, email gowen.writing@outlook.com

DANIEL 4
CONVERSION

Chapter 1
Prosperity Disturbed
(Daniel 4:1-8)[3]

An unlikely author

We begin this book by looking at one of the most remarkable chapters of the Bible. Its sixty-six books have a wide range of authors, but almost every one of them was Jewish, including Daniel. Yet here, in the middle of the book of Daniel, we have a chapter written by a Gentile. And not just *any* Gentile, but King Nebuchadnezzar, the emperor of the most powerful nation on earth at that time, a nation with the reputation of being 'the most ruthless of all nations' (Ezekiel 32:12). This was the man whose forces destroyed Jerusalem and its temple and killed or deported most of its inhabitants, Daniel included!

To appreciate how extraordinary this is, we need to realise how Jews viewed Gentiles. Throughout the period of the Bible they considered them to be beyond the pale of God's reach, unless they became Jews –

3. If you are reading the Bible in a language other than English, you may find that the division between Daniel 3 and 4 occurs in a different place. For example, in some French, German, Spanish and Italian Bibles, verses 1-3 of Daniel 4 are placed at the end of Daniel 3, so that all of the verses of Daniel 4 are three less than in this text. Almost all of the English versions which I have consulted follow the numbering that I am using; the only exception which I have been able to find is the Jerusalem Bible.

and even then they were only considered as 'converts to Judaism' (as in Acts 2:11), like second-class Jews. When Peter, a Jew, visits Cornelius the Gentile Roman centurion, even though he has had clear instructions from God to do so, he greets him rather ungraciously with the words, 'You are well aware that it is against our law for a Jew to associate with or visit a Gentile' (Acts 10:28).

When the Holy Spirit falls upon Cornelius and his Gentile friends while Peter is still preaching, he is forced to reconsider his attitude. He concludes, perhaps a little hesitantly, 'I now realise how true it is that God does not show favouritism, but accepts from every nation the one who fears him and does what is right' (Acts 10:34-35). That major worldview shift would perhaps not have been quite so difficult if he had read this chapter of the book of Daniel with unprejudiced eyes. God help us to put aside our prejudices when we read the Bible!

Next time we are tempted to write somebody off as beyond the reach of the gospel, think of Nebuchadnezzar. Outwardly he was the most unlikely person ever to turn to the living God. Yet he has the honour, given to few people, of writing a whole chapter of the Bible! After I had become a Christian, I remember one of my fellow students recounting how he had met me two weeks before my conversion. He said to himself, 'That young man will never become a Christian because he is so convinced of his own rightness.' Evidently I was able to rather effectively cover up my internal chaos with a veneer of dogmatism. Appearances can be so deceptive. And they were with Nebuchadnezzar.

As with the other chapters in the book of Daniel, the structure of this one is simple. King Nebuchadnezzar has another disturbing dream (after the one in Daniel 2), and Daniel is the only person able to interpret it for him. He disregards the warning which God gives to him through the dream and becomes absorbed in his own greatness. So God steps in and carries out the judgement which he had threatened. After seven years of insanity, the king repents, is restored to his right mind, becomes even greater than before, and praises, honours and glorifies the King of heaven.[4]

In fact, Daniel 4 is one long letter written by King Nebuchadnezzar himself. He writes it in his own everyday language, Aramaic – in contrast to the vast majority of the Old Testament, which is written in Hebrew, the language of the Jews. Because he was ruler of so many lands and peoples, he had a very wide audience; and he does not hesitate to use his status. He writes, 'To the nations and peoples of every language, who live in all the earth' (4:1).[5]

Nebuchadnezzar is totally upfront about his purpose in writing: 'It is my pleasure to tell you about the miraculous signs and wonders that the Most High God has performed for me' (4:2). This is an evangelistic letter! God has done something special for the king, and he wants the whole world to know about it – just as Peter and John told the Jewish leaders who ordered them to stop speaking in the name of Jesus, 'We cannot help speaking about what we have seen and heard' (Acts 4:18-20).

Turning now to the text of the letter, the king begins with a short hymn of praise – not in praise of his own glory, as most rulers of the time would have done (and often still do today), but in praise of the Most High God. 'How great are his signs, how mighty his wonders! His kingdom is an eternal kingdom; his dominion endures from generation to generation' (4:3). No mention of Babylonian idols. No hesitation in acknowledging the superiority of this heavenly kingdom, even over his own mighty empire.

The wonder of this chapter does not end there. For this Gentile emperor does something that would have been utterly shocking in his

4. The question may be asked, 'When did the events of Daniel 4 take place?' If you are interested in this, see Appendix C at the back of the book.

5. Where a reference is cited with only a chapter and verse number, without reference to a book, this normally refers to the book of Daniel. So, for example, this reference here is to Daniel, chapter 4, verse 1.

time. He writes about his own failings. In fact, the theme of the whole chapter is his failure to take seriously a warning from God and the consequences of it. The Babylonian Chronicles of Nebuchadnezzar's reign that have been discovered, like most official records of the time, are full of the glories of Babylon and the king's great victories in battle. Yet this chapter is so different.

That is how the Bible presents even its most heroic figures. Their achievements and their strengths are celebrated, but there is also no hesitation in bringing their weaknesses into the light. David was the greatest ever king of Israel. He conquered the whole region around Israel and exercised an influence totally disproportionate to his country's small size. Yet the biblical record does not hesitate to record his adultery with Bathsheba and arranged murder of her husband Uriah (see 2 Samuel 11 and 12), together with his song of repentance (see Psalm 51). It does not gloss over him very nearly being overthrown by his son Absalom (see 2 Samuel 15-18); nor does it ignore his disastrous census (see 1 Chronicles 21).

The New Testament continues in the same vein. Peter was the acknowledged leader of the twelve apostles and went on to become the leading apostle to the Jews and, according to tradition, the first bishop of Rome, the power centre of the day. Yet Matthew (see 16:23) records Jesus rebuking him severely; and not one of the four evangelists glosses over his threefold denial of his master while Jesus was being interrogated and mistreated (see Matthew 26:69-75; Mark 14:66-72; Luke 22:54-62; John 18:15-27).

Oliver Cromwell is famously reputed to have told the artist painting his portrait, 'Paint me with warts and all', contrary to the fashion of the time, which was to portray important people in the most flattering light.[6] The Bible portrays its characters 'with warts and all'; and Nebuchadnezzar is no exception. I find this so encouraging. I am unlikely ever to do such great things as Nebuchadnezzar, David and Peter. But God can still use me despite (or maybe because of) my weaknesses. He sees me 'warts and all', and still accepts me, just as he accepted King Nebuchadnezzar.

Reflection:

Read Nebuchadnezzar's letter in Daniel 4. What 'miraculous signs and wonders' (v. 2) can I identify in it?

Could I write a letter outlining the great things God has done for me in my life? How much would this include episodes where I failed him? Who would I send this letter to?

How might sharing my failings in my relationship with God help others to appreciate more the greatness, goodness and grace of God (see the apostle Paul's words in 1 Timothy 1:12-16)?

The complacency of prosperity

After his introduction, the king sets the scene for the events to follow: 'I, Nebuchadnezzar, was at home in my palace, contented and prosperous' (4:4). He had every reason to be contented. Daniel affirms him, 'You have become great and strong; your greatness has grown until it reaches

6. We know from his death mask that Cromwell had a prominent wart on his chin. However, the first record of a version of this phrase being used does not occur until over 100 years after his death. The full story of the phrase can be found on https://www.phrases.org.uk/meanings/warts-and-all.html.

the sky, and your dominion extends to distant parts of the earth' (4:22). Many years earlier Daniel had told him, 'You are the king of kings. The God of heaven has given you dominion and power and might and glory; in your hands he has placed all mankind and the beasts of the field and the birds in the sky. Wherever they live, he has made you ruler over them all' (2:37-38).

Nebuchadnezzar possessed all that he had ever wanted, and he could rest content in his prosperity. However, with prosperity come the temptations of complacency and self-satisfaction. Jesus exposed these in his parable of the rich man who had such a bumper harvest that he built massive barns in which to store his surplus grain, then said to himself, '"You have plenty of grain laid up for many years. Take life easy; eat, drink and be merry." But God said to him, "You fool! This very night your life will be demanded from you"' (Luke 12:16-21).

A key indicator of whether complacency has spread into a prosperous society is the way in which the poor are treated. Daniel gives only one piece of specific advice to the king after interpreting his dream: 'Renounce your sins by doing what is right, and your wickedness by *being kind to the oppressed*'[7] (4:27). The equivalent Hebrew word is often translated as 'poor', 'weak' or 'needy'. It comes to have the sense 'oppressed' because the poor, the weak and the needy are easy targets for any potential oppressor, since they lack the capacity to resist them. Despite its great wealth, it seems that there were many poor people in Babylon.

Since the end of the Second World War there has been a global surge in prosperity. World Bank data shows a phenomenal increase in global GDP[8] since 1960, from $US11 trillion to $US85 trillion (at 2010

7. Any italics in quotations from the Bible have been added by me, for emphasis. These did not exist in the original languages of the Bible.

8. Gross Domestic Product, abbreviated as GDP, is the total value of goods and services produced in a particular country or region, and so is a basic measure of its wealth.

prices) – although these riches remain very unevenly distributed. With increased wealth has come longer living: global life expectancy at birth has substantially increased over the same period, from fifty-three to seventy-three years.

Have the poor benefitted from this new prosperity? Well, the good news is that the proportion of the global population living in extreme poverty – defined as living on less than $US1.90 per day at 2011 prices – plunged spectacularly in the sixty-five years from 1950 to 2015: from 63 per cent to just 10 per cent. The bad news is that more than 700 million people in the world were still living in extreme poverty in 2015.[9] Then came the Covid pandemic; and in 2020, 115 million people had been pushed back into extreme poverty – the first such increase since 1998.[10]

How is your country handling its prosperity? If its wealth has increased, has this brought complacency and self-satisfaction? How are the poor and oppressed being treated? A good way of evaluating this is to look at the percentage of national income going to the top 10 per cent of earners: the more they take, the less there is for everybody else, especially the poorest. You can find detailed figures for your country on the World Inequality Database.[11]

I would like to spend a little time looking at the particular case of the United Kingdom, which is the country I know best. It would be worthwhile for you to research the situation for your own country and reflect on the reasons behind the trends which it has experienced in recent decades. In the UK, the accession of Mrs Thatcher as Prime Minister in 1979 heralded a long period of economic growth (after an initial recession). She confidently proclaimed that freeing the markets from bureaucratic constraints would create new wealth, which would then trickle down to all sections of the population.

---

9. https://ourworldindata.org/grapher/world-population-in-extreme-poverty-absolute.

10. https://www.bbc.co.uk/news/business-54448589.

11. https://wid.world.

However, this did not happen. As the British economy grew post-1979, so did inequality. Since then, the proportion of national income which the highest-earning 10 per cent of the population take has increased from 27 to 35 per cent. On average, each member of this privileged group now earns more than six times as much as those in the bottom-earning 50 per cent. The increase for the super-rich has been even more dramatic: the proportion of national income going to the highest-earning 1 per cent of the population has almost doubled since 1979, from 7 to 13 per cent.

This is not a party-political issue. Between 1920 and 1980 the Conservative party was in power in the UK for the majority of the time. Although they have the reputation of being the party of the economically privileged, they presided over a period when income inequality substantially diminished. On the other hand, the rise in inequality over the past forty years has taken place under both Conservative and Labour administrations. The key issue is not the colour of the party in government, but the political philosophy which it pursues and puts into action.

In fact, the idea of a trickle-down effect from economic growth was discredited more than a decade ago. In 2011 the respected newspaper, the *Financial Times* proclaimed:

> Trickle-down theory is dead. The belief fostered by Ronald Reagan in the US and Margaret Thatcher in the UK in the 1980s, that if the rich got richer their income and wealth would trickle down the income scale so that a rising tide lifted all the boats, has had the last rites pronounced on it – by the Organisation for Economic Co-operation and Development.[12]

12. https://www.ft.com/content/fba05442-1f3e-11e1-ab49-00144feabdc0.

Pope Francis sums it up admirably:

> Some people continue to defend trickle-down theories which assume that economic growth, encouraged by a free market, will inevitably succeed in bringing about greater justice and inclusiveness in the world. This opinion, which has never been confirmed by the facts, expresses a crude and naïve trust in the goodness of those wielding economic power and in the sacralized workings of the prevailing economic system. Meanwhile, the excluded are still waiting.[13]

A society's attitude to its poor is particularly exposed during a time of recession. Will the downturn disturb the complacency of the rich, putting them on the defensive? Will they attempt to hang on to their riches, so that the effects of the recession are deflected disproportionately onto the poor? Or will they make their share of the necessary sacrifices, especially for the benefit of those who were struggling to survive even before the recession hit?

When the new UK government was elected in 2010, its response to recession was to introduce austerity and to cut welfare benefits. The effects of this are graphically (and very uncomfortably) summarised by the United Nations Special Rapporteur on Extreme Poverty and Human Rights, who visited the UK in 2018. His report states:

> Although the United Kingdom is the world's fifth largest economy, one fifth of its population (14 million people) live in poverty, and 1.5 million of them experienced destitution in 2017. Policies of austerity introduced in 2010 continue largely unabated, despite the tragic social consequences.

13. Apostolic Exhortation *Evangelii Gaudium* (Libreria Editrice Vaticana, 2013), Chapter 3, p. 54.

> Close to 40 percent of children are predicted to be living in poverty by 2021. Food banks have proliferated; homelessness and rough sleeping have increased greatly; tens of thousands of poor families must live in accommodation far from their schools, jobs and community networks; life expectancy is falling for certain groups; and the legal aid system has been decimated.
>
> The social safety net has been badly damaged by drastic cuts to local authorities' budgets, which have eliminated many social services. The bottom line is that much of the glue that has held British society together since the Second World War has been deliberately removed and replaced with a harsh and uncaring ethos. A booming economy, high employment and a budget surplus have not reversed austerity, a policy pursued more as an ideological than an economic agenda.[14]

And that was before the economic devastation wrought by Covid-19!

Neglecting the poor is a sign of King Nebuchadnezzar's complacency and self-satisfaction; and God takes this very seriously. Repeatedly through his prophets he called Israel to task for their ill-treatment of the poor. Amos in particular criticises Israel for 'trampling the dust of the ground on the heads of the poor' (Amos 2:7, literal translation); for imposing a tax on the grain of the poor; for oppressing the innocent and

14. https://www.ohchr.org/EN/Issues/Poverty/Pages/CallforinputUK.aspx.
More detailed information on welfare cuts may be found in these articles:
https://www.theguardian.com/politics/2018/sep/23/welfare-spending-uk-poorest-austerity-frank-field;
https://www.independent.co.uk/news/uk/home-news/universal-credit-investment-increase-iain-duncan-smith-theresa-may-work-benefits-a8365176.html;
https://www.theguardian.com/society/2020/jul/31/universal-credit-needs-8bn-overhaul-says-cross-party-report?utm_term=f057fa3184e4a9d4bfce14a9977dfd87&utm_campaign=GuardianTodayUK&utm_source=esp&utm_medium=Email&CMP=GTUK_email.
Details of the increased use of food banks and the increase in homelessness can be found in:
https://www.trusselltrust.org/news-and-blog/latest-stats/end-year-stats/;
https://commonslibrary.parliament.uk/research-briefings/sn02007/.

taking bribes; for depriving the poor of justice in the courts (see Amos 5:11-12).

Amos then warns the rich: 'Woe to you who are complacent in Zion, and to you who feel secure on Mount Samaria. ... You lie on beds adorned with ivory and lounge on your couches. You dine on choice lambs and fattened calves. ... You drink wine by the bowlful and use the finest lotions, but you do not grieve over the ruin of Joseph. Therefore you will be among the first to go into exile; your feasting and lounging will end' (Amos 6:1-7).

Complacency and self-satisfaction act like a drug, lulling us into a false sense of security. Like a dangerous drug, it makes us feel good for a time. But we become addicted to it, and it damages our health in the long-term, though we do not notice immediately. As with Israel in Amos' day, and as with Nebuchadnezzar here, complacency and self-satisfaction lay us open to the divine displeasure. God's warning is stark. 'Whoever shuts their ears to the cry of the poor will also cry out and not be answered' (Proverbs 21:13).

Reflection:

Which sections of the population in my country are benefitting from economic prosperity, and which are not? To what extent is this disparity an issue of justice? What can I do to counter economic injustice in my country?

If I have a certain degree of economic prosperity, what are the danger signs that warn me of complacency and self-satisfaction?

How does the cry of the poor come to my ears? How can I respond to it?

Disruption

Over thirty years ago I went to hear Jim Wallis, the founder of Sojourners,[15] speak in London. There are not so many things that I heard thirty years ago that have stayed with me. But one thing he said has come back to me over and over again: 'You will know whether you are on the side of the rich or the poor by how you pray for your own situation. The rich pray for peace and the poor pray for justice.'

The rich pray for peace around them because they want to enjoy their riches with a minimum of disturbance, he said. But the poor know that there is something fundamentally wrong with their society and that justice needs to intervene. Jesus did not say, 'Blessed are those who *love* peace', or 'who *pray for* peace'; but, 'Blessed are the peace*makers*, for they will be called children of God' (Matthew 5:9). Making peace, restoring God's order to the world, will require us to confront injustice, prejudice and bigotry. It may cost us dear, as it did Jesus.

We have no record of how Nebuchadnezzar prayed before he had his dream, but it is not hard to imagine him offering sacrifices, thanking his gods for all the victories which they had brought him and praying for peace to reign in all the lands which he had conquered. However, something else was going on that he was blithely unaware of.

The Bible tells us that the role of a king is to 'deliver the needy who cry out, the afflicted who have no one to help' (Psalm 72:12). But Nebuchadnezzar did not. In marked contrast, 'the King of heaven' (4:37) 'rescues the poor from those too strong for them, the poor and needy from those who rob them' (Psalm 35:10). Nebuchadnezzar's indifference had 'caused the cry of the poor to come before God, so that he heard the cry of the needy' (Job 34:28). While he was basking in his prosperity,

---

15. Sojourners is 'a committed group of Christians who work together to live a gospel life that integrates spiritual renewal and social justice'. It began in an inner-city neighbourhood of Washington DC in 1975: https://sojo.net/biography/jim-wallis.

God had heard this cry and had decided to act – though the timing of his action would be his decision.

When God wants to rescue the poor and needy by changing an unjust status quo, he begins by bringing about, or allowing, disruption. That is what he does here with Nebuchadnezzar. The king had total control over everything around him in his waking hours. So the disruption came at the one time that he could not control: while he was asleep. He admits, 'I had a dream that made me afraid. As I was lying in bed, the images and visions that passed through my mind terrified me' (4:5).

This is what God did when he stepped in to rescue the human race from the oppression and slavery of sin (see John 8:34, Romans 6:19-20). His first step was to send an angel to disrupt the life of a Jewish teenager, Mary. She 'was greatly troubled' when the angel greeted her as a person who had 'found favour with God' – and she was even more perturbed when he told her that she would be giving birth to a baby, even though she was a virgin and not yet married (see Luke 1:26-38). The life of her fiancé, Joseph, was also seriously disrupted by the discovery that his wife-to-be was pregnant, and then again by an angel appearing in a dream to explain the pregnancy to him (see Matthew 1:20-21).

The birth of this baby began the process of releasing the Jews from the oppression of a corrupt religious system which was hindering them from knowing God (see Matthew 23:13). More than that, this process – or rather, this person, Jesus, when he became an adult – 'broke the power of him who holds the power of death – that is the devil – and freed those who all their lives were held in slavery by their fear of death' (Hebrews 2:14-15).

So, it is not surprising that there was more disruption when Mary's baby was born. 'When King Herod heard of it he was disturbed, and all Jerusalem with him' (Matthew 2:3). And the disruption did not stop there. All the boys under two years old in the Bethlehem area were slaughtered by the king in a vain attempt to eliminate his competitor. Sometimes when God intervenes, the lot of the poor and needy becomes worse before it improves.

This same process of disruption is still operating in the world, long after the Bible was completed. In the nineteenth century, under Queen Victoria, Britain enjoyed massive prosperity; yet it was still a very unequal society. Then came the disruption: on 22 January 1901 the old queen died, and Britain was greatly disturbed.

> The Queen's death - long anticipated but unexpected at the end - left Great Britain insecure and uncertain and, in some extreme cases, incredulous. Some parish clerks refused to nail the notice of her death to their church doors because they could not believe the terrible news it bore was true. Throughout most of her sixty-four glorious years, the British people had been told, by their politicians, their newspapers and their popular entertainers, that 'Victorian' was the adjective which symbolised the nation's industrial, commercial and military greatness. Now she was gone.[16]

Yet the disruption in the years following her death had many positive outcomes. A whole raft of radical new provisions for the poor were introduced, and these laid the foundations for the future welfare state: free school meals (1906), increased opportunities for poorer students to enter secondary education (1907), greater protection for vulnerable children (1908), old-age pensions (1908), labour exchanges to help the unemployed find work (1909), sickness and unemployment benefits (1911), minimum wage legislation (1913).

16. Roy Hattersley, *The Edwardians* (London: Abacus 2006), pp. 13-14.

Thirty years after these reforms, there was still widespread inequality in British society. Then came the unprecedented disruption of the Second World War. But this led to other wide-ranging welfare reforms which benefitted the whole nation, but especially the poor: the creation of the National Health Service, the provision of free compulsory secondary education for all children, and the abolition of the last vestiges of the 1834 Poor Law with its dreaded workhouses.[17]

So, with economic inequality increasing and the poor suffering – especially as a result of the Covid pandemic and the sharp rise in energy prices – we should not be surprised to see that disruption is still happening today. 'God has promised, "Once more I will shake not only the earth but also the heavens." The words "once more" indicate the removing of what can be shaken – that is, created things – so that what cannot be shaken may remain. Therefore, since we are receiving a kingdom that cannot be shaken, let us be thankful, and so worship God acceptably with reverence and awe' (Hebrews 12:26-28).

Reflection:

Do I find myself praying more for peace or for justice in my own life situation? Why is this?

Where do I see disruption taking place today – in my locality, in my country, or globally? How is God at work through this disruption? How can I pray into situations of disruption?

17. Workhouses were officially abolished in 1930, but many of them continued to be run for a number of years by local authorities as Public Assistance Institutions, especially outside London.

When things around me are being shaken, what can I hold on to that cannot be shaken?

Confusion and turmoil

Disruption very often brings confusion and turmoil in its wake, because some of the fixed points that we have trusted in have been shaken or are no longer there. We can feel like the sailors in the boat caught in the storm during the apostle Paul's journey to Rome: 'When neither sun nor stars [fixed points] appeared for many days and the storm continued raging, we finally gave up all hope' (Acts 27:20).

When Nebuchadnezzar's prosperity and complacency were disrupted by his dream, he too was confused. He followed the standard procedure by calling together all his magicians, enchanters, astrologers and diviners, but not one of them could clear up the confusion and interpret the dream for him (see 4:7).

We saw in the previous section how Mary was 'greatly troubled' by the angel's greeting; and she was confused too. She scratched her head and 'wondered what kind of greeting this might be' (Luke 1:29). And we can imagine the confusion and turmoil going through Joseph's mind as he tried to equate the exemplary character of the woman he knew and respected with the fact that she was pregnant.

Moving forward in time, we saw how Queen Victoria's death was so disturbing to Britain. That disturbance heralded a decade of political turmoil in Britain, with the House of Lords finally surrendering its right to block legislation after a long, drawn-out battle. Then came the turmoil of the First World War, where millions died or were wounded.

More recently, the disruption of the 1956 Suez Crisis led to a decade of confusion and turmoil around Britain's role in the world. Prime Minister Anthony Eden resigned after less than two years in office.

The British Empire began to disintegrate, as colony after colony was granted independence. Then Britain effectively ended her role as a global military power in 1967 when Prime Minister Harold Wilson announced her withdrawal from her major South-east Asian bases and her abandonment of any special military role east of Suez.

If we want to know where God is at work in the world today, the presence of confusion and turmoil is often a good indicator. 'God is not a God of disorder' (1 Corinthians 14:33). So, he is not the author of turmoil and confusion. However, he uses for his own purposes the turmoil and confusion that arises from the world being out of sync with how he created it. This may not be immediately obvious, and we may have to search for the evidence before we find it.

For example, in Syria, prior to the outbreak of the civil war in 2011, Christians were largely left alone by the government to practise their religion in peace, but very few Muslims ever came to faith in Christ. Since the disruption, confusion and turmoil of the war, there has been a flood of Muslims converting to Christianity. I heard one Syrian pastor, who had stayed with his church in Damascus, tell how two-thirds of his church had left the country, but the church was still full; most of those attending were Muslim-background believers. Another pastor in Aleppo asked Christians at one point not to attend all of the Sunday services so as to make room for Muslim enquirers.

In India, persecution of Christians has intensified since the Bharatiya Janata Party came to power in 2014. Radical Hindu movements have the express aim of driving out from India all religions other than Hinduism. Despite the confusion and turmoil which this has brought, the Christian Church is growing, and has done so even under the coronavirus lockdown.[18]

---

18. See, for example, www.christianitytoday.com/ct/2020/april-web-only/india-churches-covid-19-coronavirus-pandemic-lockdown.html.

It can take confusion and turmoil to break down barriers which have been built up over generations and to create an openness to the good news of Jesus Christ. But there needs to be a functioning Church to point people towards that good news; otherwise they fall into despair and hopelessness, like the sailors with the apostle Paul. Afghanistan, for example, has experienced fifty years of turmoil and internal conflict since King Mohammed Zahir Shah was deposed in 1973. But there are so few Afghan Christians to proclaim the good news of Jesus Christ – and most of them are isolated, secret believers – that Afghans troubled by turmoil and confusion remain in despair.

Nebuchadnezzar was more fortunate than the Afghans. In his confusion he was able to turn to Daniel, whom he seems to have kept in reserve for the very hardest problems. He was still wedded to his gods, for he refers to Daniel by his Babylonian name, Belteshazzar, adding, 'He's named after my god' (4:7-8, paraphrase). But a lot more was going on under the surface, as we shall see presently.

Reflection:

Where do I see turmoil and confusion in my own country today? Where do I see it in the wider world? What barriers is the turmoil and confusion breaking down?

What can I discern God doing in the midst of that turmoil and confusion? How can I pray into it?

Chapter 2
Unexpected Revelation
(Daniel 4:9-19)

Exercising spiritual gifts

I remember a group of us travelling in a couple of Land Cruisers from South Sudan to reach a remote community in north-eastern Democratic Republic of the Congo. The roads were passable, though very bumpy. Suddenly we found a tree had fallen across the road and was blocking any further progress. We could not go off-road around it, as the terrain on either side of the road was too unstable. While we Europeans scratched our heads wondering what to do, the Africans leapt out of their vehicles and set to work with their machetes.

It was wonderful to behold. Within a few minutes and with many powerful machete blows, they completely stripped the tree of all its branches, so that we only had to roll the trunk of the tree away from the road. Then we could continue our journey. Here was an emergency. Our African friends had their machetes well honed, so they were equal to the emergency and were able to use them to good effect and so allow us to move forward.

That is how it is with spiritual gifts. Daniel was facing an emergency: the king was desperate to know what his dream meant; and who could tell what he might do if his desire was not satisfied? Daniel had spent time developing and practising his gift of understanding mysteries and interpreting dreams; and the king recognised this (see 4:9). So, when the time came for him to use his gift urgently, it was well-honed and ready to be employed (like my African friends' machetes). For he seems to have received the interpretation of the king's dream almost immediately (see 4:19).

Since Daniel's exercise of his spiritual gifts plays such an important role in both Daniel 4 and Daniel 5, it is worth taking a moment to examine how we can effectively exercise ours.

Exercising a spiritual gift always requires faith. Daniel needed a good deal of faith to give the king a very uncomfortable message (see 4:19-27). Take the example of prophecy. I may feel that I have received a prophetic word for a particular person; but I will never know whether or not it is accurate unless I exercise faith and speak it out. If I do, and it proves to be spot on, that increases my confidence and faith for future occasions. It sets up a virtuous circle: accuracy leads to more confident prophecy, leads to more accuracy, leads to still more confident prophecy, and so on.

If, however, my prophetic word turns out to be wide of the mark in some way, then the temptation is to say, 'That's it. I knew my prophetic gift was really weak. Maybe I don't have one at all. I'm not going to prophesy again.' Such discouragement never comes from God, but from the devil. If my heart is open to instruction, I can learn a lot from my failures.

An arrow is only sharp when it has been honed, and this requires the removal of material from the tip. God often needs to take things away from us, through failure, to hone our spiritual gifts: maybe our pride, or our need to be right. Our weakness arising from failure, under God's direction can become a source of strength (see 2 Corinthians 12:9). We only have Daniel's accurate interpretations recorded in the Bible; but quite probably he too had a number of failures along the way as he learned to develop his gifts.

The spiritual gifts which God gives to us are many and varied. There are lists in the New Testament in Romans 12:6-8, 1 Corinthians 12:7-11 and Ephesians 4:7-13, but none of these is exhaustive. For example, none of them mentions dream interpretation. Nor do we find in them Daniel's gift of 'knowledge and understanding of all kinds of literature and learning' (1:17). That gift is still being used powerfully by God, as we see, for example, from the life of C.S. Lewis. He was so gifted that he became Professor of Medieval and Renaissance Literature at the University of Cambridge. And he used his gift in writings that have profoundly influenced several generations of Christians – and continue to do so, long after his death in 1963.

Spiritual gifts have a powerful role to play in the Church. 'To each one the manifestation of the Spirit is given for the common good' (1 Corinthians 12:7) – the common good of the Christian community, as the context makes clear. God has given gifts 'to equip his people for works of service, so that the body of Christ may be built up' (Ephesians 4:12). From verses such as these we might conclude that the Church is the only place for spiritual gifts to be used.

However, as I reflected on Daniel's experience, I realised that I needed to broaden my perspective. Had he limited himself to exercising his spiritual gifts in a believing community, he would never have used them – because no such community existed in the royal court of Babylon. However, we find him regularly using his gifts in those pagan surroundings: interpreting dreams here and in Daniel 2, interpreting a mysterious sign from God in Daniel 5, and receiving a series of prophetic revelations in Daniel 7-12. From the testimony of Belshazzar's mother in 5:10-12, it is clear that many people in the royal court were aware of his gifts, and that he had gained a considerable reputation.

Had I looked more carefully at the life of Jesus, I would have seen that he reinforced this lesson. He was the most spiritually gifted person ever to live on earth. Unlike Daniel, he grew up in a society where there was a strong believing community. Yet he exercised his spiritual gifts – teaching, healing, driving out demons, raising the dead, prophesying and many more – mostly outside the synagogue and the temple (the places where the believing community gathered in those days). Often he used his gifts to benefit people whom the Jewish religious leaders despised and had written off: the woman with a haemorrhage of blood, who was excluded as unclean (see Luke 8:43-48); a Samaritan woman ostracised even by her own community (see John 4); the tax-collector Zacchaeus (see Luke 19:1-10).

Jesus explains why he operated in this way: 'I was sent only to the *lost sheep* of Israel' (Matthew 15:24), many of whom felt so lost that they would not dared to have entered a synagogue or the temple. 'It is not the healthy who need a doctor, but those who are ill. I have not come to call the righteous, but sinners', he declared (Mark 2:17).

Wherever Christians today are copying Jesus' example, they are seeing God's power at work in a way that is rarely seen inside the Church. Some churches engage regularly in Healing on the Streets.[19] They set up a stall in the main street of their town and invite passers-by to receive prayer if they have physical, emotional or mental ailments. And they see many marvellous healings take place. Praying for one another in church is important; and I have seen many wonderful healings in church over the years. However, when prayer for healing is taken outside the Church, it seems to ratchet it up several levels.

This is not a new idea. William Temple, Archbishop of Canterbury during the Second World War, is widely credited with saying (though nobody is quite sure where), 'The Church is the only society that exists for the benefit of those who are not its members.' Around the same time, Dietrich Bonhoeffer, a German pastor executed by Hitler in 1945,

19. See https://www.healingonthestreets.com.

said, 'The Church is the Church only when it exists for others, ... not dominating, but helping and serving.'[20]

A great deal of effort is required to maintain a church and its regular activities; and that maintenance can easily become the overall goal. The attention of its members can easily turn inwards, with their focus on those outside the church growing dim. I heard John Wright, National Director of Vineyard Churches UK & Ireland, at the April 2021 Vineyard National Gathering, compare this to a game of chess. The queen is the most powerful piece on the board, but novice players often make the mistake of using her too much, and they do not sufficiently develop the other pieces. So, while they are being trained, they are sometimes required to play a game without the queen on the board.

Covid-19 took away churches' most powerful piece, the queen – that is, our Sunday services. We have had to learn to develop the other pieces – which include reaching out to and serving the world and using our spiritual gifts outside the church. Nevertheless, as John reminded us, we should never forget that the game is not about the queen, or any other piece, but about the King.

Reflection:

How do I keep my spiritual gifts well honed?

What have I learned from failures in the exercise of my spiritual gifts? How do I avoid being discouraged by these failures?

What initiative could I take the to exercise my spiritual gifts in places outside the Church?

20. Dietrich Bonhoeffer, *Letters and Papers from Prison* (London: Fontana, 1951).

Disturbing clarity

The king recounts his dream to Daniel (see 4:10-18). He saw a massive tree, providing shelter and food to all kinds of animals and birds. Then a heavenly messenger takes centre stage. He first calls for the tree to be stripped and cut down, leaving the stump and its roots, bound with iron and bronze. Then the messenger utters the enigmatic words, 'Let him be drenched with the dew of heaven, and let him live with the animals among the plants of the earth. Let his mind be changed from that of a man and let him be given the mind of an animal, till seven times pass by for him' (4:15-16).

The messenger concludes by saying that the events of the dream are 'so that the living may know that the Most High is sovereign over all kingdoms on earth and gives them to anyone he wishes and sets over them the lowliest of people' (4:17). The lessons of this dream are for 'the living', not just for King Nebuchadnezzar – and that includes all of us who are reading this.

After confusion and turmoil comes clarity; but that clarity can bring its own turmoil and disturbance. As the king is speaking, Daniel's confusion and turmoil begins to clear, and clarity comes to him. But that clarity brings with it a disturbing realisation. He was 'greatly perplexed for a time, and his thoughts terrified him' (4:19). For it dawns on him that the massive, fruitful tree that is cut down in the dream is the king himself. This dream is warning Nebuchadnezzar that there is a real danger of his kingship being taken away from him.

Just as Queen Victoria's reign brought wealth and stability to Britain in the nineteenth century, so Nebuchadnezzar had brought prosperity, stability and a sense of security to Babylon. Now, God was warning, all that was about to be turned upside down. No wonder that Daniel was perplexed and terrified. There was no visible chink in Nebuchadnezzar's armour. He was in total control of his empire. All aspirants to his throne had been eliminated. How could it be possible for God to bring about such a dramatic and devastating change? What awful things would the king have to experience? What would happen to Babylon if his reassuring presence was no longer there? Who would take over from him? Would they be up to the job? And what would happen to Daniel's own position?

The deeper the revelation we receive from God, the more disturbing it may be. Daniel is one of many people in the Bible who received clarity that led to disturbance. The apostle Peter received from God a depth of revelation that nobody had ever experienced before: that Jesus was the Christ, 'the Son of the living God'. He was delighted to have Jesus' affirmation (Matthew 16:15-20) and we can imagine him saying, 'Right, Jesus, now we've cleared up who you are, let's get going on your messianic mission! No time to lose!'

Instead, Jesus gives Peter and the disciples a still deeper, but very disturbing revelation – not at all what they were expecting. He 'began to explain to his disciples that he must go to Jerusalem and suffer many things at the hands of the elders, the chief priests and the teachers of the law, and that he must be killed and on the third day be raised to life.' So perturbed was Peter by this that he tried to dissuade Jesus away from it; and he was strongly rebuked (Matthew 16:21-23).

Just six days later, Peter, along with James and John, receives a unique revelation of Jesus' glory on a high mountain. 'Surely this must be it,' we can hear him saying to himself. 'With that kind of glory, we can take on the world! Nobody will be able to resist us.' But when they get down from the mountain, once again Jesus gives the disciples disturbing revelation about him suffering, dying and being raised from the dead (see Matthew 17:1-13). That was definitely not part of the disciples' plan for him!

Another person who had a similar experience was the Jewish prophet Habakkuk, who lived not long before Daniel. During a troubled period in his country's history, he questions the Lord as to why justice has not been done in relation to the destruction, violence, strife and conflict that he sees everywhere around him. It is the same question people in many countries of the world might be asking today.

The reply which Habakkuk receives is clear, but it is also profoundly disturbing. The Lord tells him that he will make sure that justice is done towards Judah, where Habakkuk lived, but it will be by the hands of the Babylonians, who were notorious for their ruthlessness. 'But they are worse than we are!' Habakkuk bemoans. 'Where is the justice there?' (see Habakkuk 1). The Lord takes the prophet's new question seriously, and his answer is given in Habakkuk 2. He says, in summary, 'Yes, I will deal with the Babylonians too, but I will do it in my own time and in my own way.'

Is it OK to ask the Lord questions about revelation which we have received and which disturbs us? It all depends on the spirit in which we ask. For example, an angel came to Zechariah to tell him that his wife would be having a baby, even though she was many years past the menopause. His response, 'How can I be sure of this?' came from unbelief. So he was struck dumb until he publicly demonstrated his faith by insisting that the newborn baby be called John, as the angel had instructed him (Luke 1:11-22,57-66).

Six months later (as we saw earlier), Mary also received an angelic visitor telling her about a pregnancy: her own. Her questioning response, 'How will this be ... since I am a virgin?' on the surface looks to be the same as Zechariah's. But hers came from a position of faith. She was genuinely confused at how a baby could be planted in her body without a man being involved. So the angel honours her faith by explaining that, instead of a man planting his seed in her, the Holy Spirit, 'the power of the Most High' would do it (Luke 1:26-38).

Her question was answered with clarity, but the consequences of the revelation were still highly disturbing for her. She and Joseph would be ostracised by family and friends, so much so that not one of them was prepared to take them into their home in Bethlehem when she was about to give birth. A lifelong shadow was cast over her reputation. Even thirty years later, when Jesus was an adult, people were still disparagingly calling him 'Mary's son' (Mark 6:3).

Reflection:

When have I received revelation – for myself or for somebody else – that has disturbed me? What did I do, or am doing, in response to that disturbance?

Are there situations where I am reluctant to ask God for clarity because, deep down, I fear that his answer may disturb me? Which of the examples from the Bible in this section do I find might help me in this?

If I am questioning God about something, how do I know whether my question is based on faith or unbelief?

Chapter 3
Rebuke
(Daniel 4:20-27)

The art of rebuke

Daniel is standing before the most powerful ruler in the world, a man who could promote people or have them executed with just one word. The king is hanging on Daniel's every word. How can he be told that the dream is a warning to him that, if he does not change his ways, he risks losing his kingdom and suffering insanity for seven years?

It is unlikely that you or I will ever be put in such a precarious position. Yet many of us may be faced with a situation where we sense God prompting us to warn somebody about the dangers of a certain course of action which they may be taking or are about to take. It could be a friend, a work colleague, a family member, perhaps even our boss or a church leader.

What am I to do? What does it look like to be faithful to God in that situation? Should I wait for some confirmation before I say anything, or should I take my courage in both hands and speak out? Would it be better to just pray for the person on the lines that God had shown me? Should I risk damaging our relationship by speaking out? Would I sound presumptuous if I said what I felt God had given to me?

The Bible has much to say about rebuke, especially in the book of Proverbs, which is designed to align our conduct with God's wisdom. In that book the Hebrew noun for 'rebuke' (which in some English versions may be translated as 'reproof', 'correction', 'warning' or 'reprimand') occurs sixteen times and the corresponding verb ten times.[21] For example, 'Whoever rebukes a person will in the end gain favour rather than one who has a flattering tongue' (Proverbs 28:23).

So, are we at liberty to rebuke anybody and everybody? First of all, let us heed Jesus' warning, 'Do not judge, or you too will be judged' (Matthew 7:1). Rebuke can easily turn into judgement. Jesus exhorts us not to be preoccupied about removing the speck of sawdust from our brother's eye when we have a plank of wood stuck in our own eye. He calls that hypocrisy (see Matthew 7:3-5). Before we engage in rebuke, self-examination is necessary. How does our own life measure up in the area of the rebuke? What is in our heart towards the other person?

A word of rebuke works best in the context of a relationship of trust, so that the person receiving the rebuke feels confident that we are doing it with their best interests at heart. It is also helpful if we have a track record of wisdom and discernment. Daniel had served Nebuchadnezzar for at least twenty years by this time. The king knew that he had his best interests at heart and that (as he put it), 'the spirit of the holy gods' was in him (4:18). Proverbs 27:5 says, 'Better is open rebuke than hidden love', implying that genuine rebuke comes from a position of love. The verse following it is even clearer, 'Wounds *from a friend* can be trusted'.

There are instances in the Bible where a person is given a direct mandate from God to rebuke a person who they did not know, such as the unnamed man of God from Judah who rebuked King Jeroboam while he was sacrificing to his idols on his freshly built altar (see 1 Kings 13). But these are rather rare; and in that particular case there were powerful confirmatory signs to show the king that the rebuke was from

21. The noun *tōkhachath* occurs in Proverbs 1:23,25,30; 3:11; 5:12; 6:23; 10:17; 12:1; 13:18; 15:5,10,31,32; 27:5; 29:1,15. The verb from which it derives, *yākhach*, is in Proverbs 3:12; 9:7; 9:8 (twice); 15:12; 19:25; 24:25; 25:12; 28:23; 30:6.

God. The altar 'split apart', its ashes were poured out on the ground, Jeroboam's arm withered when he ordered the man to be seized, then it was healed when the prophet interceded for him.

Likewise, Jesus rebuked a lame man whom he had not previously met, telling him to stop a particular (unnamed) sin, else he would end up in a worse state. But that was after he had given the man a powerful sign, healing him instantly from thirty-eight years of immobility (see John 5:1-15). After experiencing a sign like that, the man was no doubt very open to listening to the rebuke!

If we are praying for somebody who is not well known to us and we feel that we need to say something difficult to them on the lines of a rebuke, it is well worth seeking advice from trusted Christian friends. We might also ask God for some kind of confirmation: for example, a relevant piece of information about the person's life which we could not have otherwise known; or a Bible verse that speaks into their situation; or an unexpected encounter with them.

A friend of mine was at a large Christian conference and had a clear impression that one of the speakers was struggling with a serious, highly delicate issue in his life, and God was calling him to sort it out. Given the sensitivity of the matter, my friend knew he needed confirmation of some kind. So he prayed that, if he was to say something, he would come face to face with this person without anybody else being around – quite a big ask in a conference of several thousand people. But not too big for God! Sure enough, the next day as he was returning to his chalet, he 'happened' to bump into this person, with nobody else in sight. He knew then that he had to pass on the rebuke that God had shown him.

Sometimes God gives us information about a person and wants us to pray for them without confronting them. At a time when I was responsible for coordinating the home groups in my church, I felt I received a disturbing revelation from God that the lifestyle of one of the home group leaders was not at all in line with Jesus' teaching. What was I to do? Should I go and rebuke them? I decided to seek the advice of my minister. He told me that he had received exactly the same revelation, but he also felt strongly that he was to pray about it and not confront the person. So we both prayed, and six months later the person left the church for no particular reason and was never seen again. If we try to rebuke when we have no mandate from God to do so, it will be ineffective, even harmful. Let us follow Jesus' example: 'Whatever I say is just what the Father has told me to say' (John 12:50).

In fact, Daniel had no option but to rebuke the king. For he had explicitly said to him, 'Tell me what the dream means' (see 4:18). So, either he lied and softened up the interpretation - which would have seriously compromised his integrity and his faithfulness to God - or he gave the king the whole uncomfortable truth. Then, the consequences, and his life, were in God's hands.

Reflection:

When did I take the decision to rebuke somebody? What motivated me to do this? What factors did I take into consideration before deciding to rebuke? What counsel did I receive from other people?

How would I assess the outcome of my rebuke? With the benefit of hindsight, are there any ways in which I might have acted differently?

Thinking of a time when I was rebuked by somebody, how did I feel at the time? How did the way in which the rebuke was given influence my (positive or negative) response to it?

Life-giving rebuke

Proverbs 15:31 states, 'Whoever heeds life-giving correction [same Hebrew word as 'rebuke'] will be at home among the wise.' A rebuke is meant to bring life. If it is to achieve this, there are four pitfalls to avoid; and we see Daniel avoiding each one of them.

Firstly, rebuke must not be confused with criticism or complaint. Rebuke is given with a focus on the good of the person to whom we are speaking – just as Daniel's major concern was that the king responded well to the rebuke (see 4:27). Criticism and complaint are more focused on *me*, on what *I* would like to see changed, on what *I* am not happy with – although, of course, we can wrap this up in spiritual language and claim to be speaking in God's name or serving his best interests.

Daniel's rebuke ultimately brought true spiritual life to the king, even though it took eight years. Criticism and complaint are never life-giving, but life-sapping. All leaders have to deal with them, especially church leaders. I have found that persistent criticism of my church leadership, more than anything else, has drained life from me and worn me down over a period of time.

There is a temptation for leaders to harden themselves against any and every criticism. I remember hearing the widow of a prominent church leader say, after her husband had died, that people said to her that he must have had a really thick skin to cope with all the criticism he received; but that wasn't so, she would reply; it really affected him. As leaders, we need to allow criticism to get to us to some extent; otherwise we risk becoming immunised against genuine rebuke, which can lead to arrogance.

Personalised criticism is particularly destructive: accusations such as, '*You are* such and such a kind of person'; '*You are not* fit to lead'; '*You don't* care.' I have found that criticism of this kind opens up avenues for demonic forces to attack you. I remember asking myself, after one particularly difficult episode of personalised criticism, why it had affected me so deeply. Then I realised that it had been a vehicle for demonic attack.

That had almost certainly not been the intention of my critics. However, they had unwittingly opened themselves up to being a channel for demonic influence, which was destructive for me, and probably for them too. Jesus warns of this danger: 'Anyone who says to a brother or sister ... "You fool!" [personalised criticism] will be in danger of the fire of hell' (Matthew 5:22). Hell is the domain of the devil; and Jesus is not talking only about our eternal destiny, but about consequences here and now.

The apostle Paul confirms this. He tells the Corinthian church, 'You yourselves are God's temple and ... God's Spirit lives among you. If anyone destroys God's temple [whether through personalised criticism or any other means], God will destroy that person; for God's temple is sacred and you together are that temple' (1 Corinthians 3:16-17). These are solemn words. If we criticise destructively, we open ourselves to destructive forces. So, before we open our mouths to rebuke a fellow Christian, we should reflect carefully on whether our words will build up or tear down (see 2 Corinthians 10:8; 13:10).

The second pitfall is allowing our rebuke to become harsh, even judgemental. We will be especially prone to this temptation if we are speaking about an issue which we ourselves are also struggling with. For we tend to be most intolerant of the faults in others that we are aware of in ourselves. Although we may convince ourselves that we are demonstrating the righteous anger of God in what we are saying, anger is much more likely to be rooted in our own self. And 'human anger does not produce the righteousness that God desires' (James 1:20).

Notice the way in which Daniel speaks to the king before he delivers his devastating interpretation. There is not a hint of harshness, not a trace of human anger, although the way in which Nebuchadnezzar ran his empire could have given Daniel plenty to be angry about. Rather, he says, 'My lord, if only the dream applied to your enemies and its meaning to your adversaries!' (4:19).

It is always useful to examine our hearts and ask in what spirit we are giving a word of rebuke or correction. Are we venting our own anger? Are we taking the opportunity to put the person down or shame them? Are we concealing our real feelings and motives under a cloak of concern for God's righteousness? If a rebuke is given out of love for the person, even if it is given awkwardly, 'Love covers over a multitude of sins' (1 Peter 4:8). The apostle Paul sums it up well: 'Brothers and sisters, if someone is caught in a sin, you who live by the Spirit should restore that person *gently*. But watch yourselves, or you also may be tempted' (Galatians 6:1).

The third pitfall is to give rebuke without offering the person a way out of their situation. This amounts to condemnation; and 'there is now no condemnation for those who are in Christ Jesus' (Romans 8:1). So, the aim is not to dump on the other person our feelings about what they are doing or have done wrong, but to offer them a way out, just as God offers a way of escape from every temptation that comes to us (see 1 Corinthians 10:13).

The prophet Nathan had a very severe rebuke to give to King David for his adultery and murder. But as soon as he acknowledges his sin, Nathan gives him the comforting word, 'The LORD has taken away your sin. You are not going to die' (2 Samuel 12:13). Likewise, Daniel offers Nebuchadnezzar a way of avoiding the threatened punishment. 'Your Majesty, be pleased to accept my advice: renounce your sins by doing what is right, and your wickedness by being kind to the oppressed. It may be that then your prosperity will continue' (4:27). In dealing with a disciplinary situation as a leader, especially in a church, a plan for the person's restoration should always be formulated.

Reflection:

When have I experienced or witnessed the destructive power of personalised criticism? What effect did it have on the person giving and on the person receiving the criticism?

Which of these three pitfalls has spoken most to me, and why? Can I identify a situation where I fell (or nearly fell) into that pitfall when rebuking somebody?

How will awareness of this pitfall change the way in which I handle rebuke in the future?

To rebuke or not to rebuke?

The final pitfall when rebuking is opposite to the other three. It is the temptation *not* to rebuke: to say nothing, or to dilute what you feel you ought to say. How easy it is to duck out of speaking that difficult word to a friend, to our boss at work, to a church leader, to some other authority figure. Fear of how a rebuke will affect our reputation, our future prospects or our future relationships can so easily paralyse us. This would have been the path of least resistance for Daniel. If the king had been upset with his words, he could have ordered his immediate execution. So there must have been a strong temptation to water down what God had given him, to conceal or gloss over the most negative aspects. But he did not. He remained faithful to God.

The other day I was speaking with a friend who was fairly new in his company and had challenged his Chief Executive Officer about an instruction that he had given. 'Nobody had ever challenged the CEO before,' he said, 'but I really felt that what he wanted done was not in the best interests of the company.' He gave the rebuke in a tactful and private manner, and made clear that if the CEO insisted on maintaining his position, he would still follow his instructions. The CEO did accept what he said. What shocked him (and me) was that nobody before in the company had ever had the courage to do this.

Christians are especially susceptible to this trap, for we may feel that being Christlike means always being encouraging and saying positive things. Another friend told me about his boss, the chief executive of a Christian organisation. When he came back from a business trip abroad with several other staff members, he complained bitterly to him that all the engagements and responsibilities during the trip had fallen on him and the other members of the team had not pulled their weight. But during the trip he had stayed silent and had not rebuked them over their non-participation.

In Belgium, from my own experience, British people have the reputation of being moaners but not complainers. For example, if a Belgian is served an unsatisfactory meal in a restaurant, it is most likely that they will send it back. A British person in the same situation is more likely to eat the meal then moan about it to their friends afterwards. So, British people may be particularly open to the temptation not to rebuke, but to stay silent and moan to somebody else about the person whom they should have rebuked.

One final remark on this subject. We are responsible for the way in which we give a rebuke, but not for the way in which the person responds to it. The fact that Daniel stayed alive, even though he had accused the king of sins and wickedness, shows that Nebuchadnezzar listened carefully to his interpretation of the dream. However, he did not act on it. As the dream began to fade from his mind, his complacency returned. For twelve months life in the royal palace continued as normal (see 4:29).

It took eight years, after seven years of isolation and insanity, before Nebuchadnezzar took Daniel's advice, repented and gave his life to praising, exalting and glorifying 'the King of heaven' (see 4:37). Daniel had to be patient. Even when the king's insanity began, as God had foretold, he could still not be completely sure how long the 'seven times' of the dream would last.[22] He needed to hear the same words that the Lord would later speak in response to Habakkuk's questioning: 'The revelation awaits an appointed time; it … will not prove false. Though it linger, wait for it; it will certainly come and will not delay' (Habakkuk 2:3).

Waiting for revelation to come into being can be very challenging. After the event, when it has happened, everything looks so obvious. But the waiting period is hard. Maintaining a long-term perspective will help us not to be discouraged. 'Perseverance produces character; and character, hope' (Romans 5:4).

Reflection:

Reflecting on a situation where I had to decide whether or not to give a word of rebuke to somebody, what factors influenced my decision?

If I had to take a similar decision today, would there be other factors which I would take into account?

22. We do not know the precise length of the 'seven times' referred to in 4:16, 23, 25 and 32. They might refer to an unspecified period of time being completed, seven being the number of completeness in the Bible (e.g. seven days of creation; the furnace heated seven times hotter, 3:19; seven days in a week). The general consensus is that they represent seven years, but the exact length of time is not material. We know that it was long enough for the king to have been set aside from his throne (4:31) and to grow hair 'like the feathers of an eagle' and 'nails like the claws of a bird' (4:33).

Can I think of a situation where I moaned about a person to somebody else, but did not speak to that person directly about the issue? How do I feel about that now?

Can I think of a situation where I moaned about a person to somebody else, but did not speak to that person directly about the issue? How do I feel about that now?

Chapter 4
Fall, But ...
(Daniel 4:28-33)

Pride and fall

Jonathan Aitken was a British cabinet minister who was being tipped as a future leader of the Conservative Party. In 1999 his world fell apart when, after a high-profile court case, he was convicted of perjury, served a prison term and was declared bankrupt.

He had presented himself as a knight in shining armour exposing the cesspit of the media by bringing a libel action against *The Guardian* newspaper. Instead of being vindicated, this set in motion events that led to his criminal conviction. He had proclaimed loudly and publicly, 'If it falls to me to start a fight to cut out the cancer of bent and twisted journalism in our country with the simple Sword of Truth and the trusty Shield of British Fair Play, so be it. I am ready for the fight.'[23] However, his 'Sword of Truth' quickly turned into what the media then dubbed a 'Dagger of Deceit'.

Aitken subsequently wrote a book, reviewing with considerable frankness the events which had led to his conviction. He recounts how becoming a Christian completely changed his perspective. Towards the end of the book, he shares how for a long time he had felt himself

23. https://www.theguardian.com/theguardian/from-the-archive-blog/2011/jun/06/newspapers-national-newspapers.

to be the victim of a media conspiracy, of bad luck, of unfortunate circumstances. Then an awful realisation dawned on him:

> Pride was the root cause of all my evils. Without pride there would have been no libel action, no attempt to defend the Ritz bill payment with a lie; no will to win the battle in court on an ends-justifies-the-means basis. There would have been no deceit of friends, family and colleagues; no Sword of Truth speech; no involvement of my wife and daughter in the front line of the war with *The Guardian*. If I had been blessed with a small helping of humility instead of possessed by a surfeit of pride, the entire tragedy would have been avoided. ... My pride had been such a powerful, blinding, demonic state of mind that could only be cured by the severest of lessons.[24]

Daniel was well aware of Nebuchadnezzar's pride, but tactfully refers to it only obliquely in his advice to the king. 'Renounce your sins by doing what is right, and your wickedness by being kind to the oppressed', he advises (4:27). 'Renouncing your sins', admitting that you have been wrong and need to change, deals a hefty blow to your pride.

Jesus' first public proclamation was, 'The kingdom of God has come near. Repent and believe the good news!' (Mark 1:15). The command to repent, in the original Greek, is in the present continuous tense, which has the sense, 'Keep on repenting'. Repentance is the entry point into the kingdom of God; but it is not only for our conversion. Sin 'so easily entangles' us (Hebrews 12:1). Repentance disentangles us. Remaining entangled in our sins and our pride encumbers us with a burden that is so large that it stops us from passing through the narrow gate (see Matthew 7:13-14).

24. Jonathan Aitken, *Pride and Perjury* (London: Harper Collins, 2000), p. 358.

Repentance is the bedrock of our Christian faith. Martin Luther, whose famous *95 Theses* sparked the European Reformation, understood this very well. The very first one of those theses, written in 1517, states, 'When our Lord and Master Jesus Christ said, "Repent", he willed the entire life of believers to be one of repentance.'[25]

We mentioned earlier how pleased Peter was when Jesus affirmed his confession that he was the Christ, 'the Son of the living God' (Matthew 16:16). He was not only pleased, but proud – so proud that he took it upon himself to rebuke Jesus for daring to suggest that he was going to suffer and die in Jerusalem. 'Pride goes before destruction, a haughty spirit before a fall' (Proverbs 16:18). Peter's fall was sudden and dramatic. Jesus rebuked him in the most severe manner in front of all the other disciples: 'Get behind me, Satan! You are a stumbling-block to me' (Matthew 16:21-23).

Even that did not cure Peter's pride. It is often so deeply rooted within us. A few days later, Jesus warned his disciples that he was about to be arrested and they would all be scattered. Peter, however, was having none of that, and insisted, 'Even if all fall away on account of you, I never will' (Matthew 26:31-33). His self-confidence, rooted in pride (as self-confidence invariably is), was quickly shattered. Soon after his show of bravado, he denied even knowing Jesus on three separate occasions (see Matthew 26:69-75). When Jesus comes to restore him after his resurrection, in John 21:15-19, we can see how that self-confidence and pride has been broken.

Few of us may have such a dramatic fall as Jonathan Aitken or Peter – or Nebuchadnezzar. But any one of us can be seriously harmed by pride. So often it works its destructive power without us being aware. C.S. Lewis wisely observed:

---

25. https://www.luther.de/en/95thesen.html.

> There is one vice of which no man in the world is free; which every one in the world loathes when he sees it in someone else; and of which hardly any people, except Christians, ever imagine that they are guilty themselves. ... There is no fault which makes a man more unpopular, and no fault which we are more unconscious of in ourselves. ...The vice I am talking of is Pride.[26]

Just as C.S. Lewis says, Nebuchadnezzar never imagined that he was guilty of pride. We are not told how he reacted to Daniel's words. They must have had some positive impact on him, because Daniel stayed alive. Perhaps the king took them to heart at first, or reflected on them. But when nothing happened over several months, they began to fade away into the background. How easy it is to forget what God has said to us. It does not have to be deliberate; his words can just slip out of our consciousness over a period of time.

That is what seems to have happened with Nebuchadnezzar. For, only twelve months after receiving the warning from the dream, we find him walking on the roof of the royal palace, admiring the fruit of his grandiose building projects. New building projects are a sign of life and dynamism in a city. That was how it was in Brussels for the twenty-five years that we lived there. The European quarter was almost a permanent building site in one part or another. That gave a feeling of, 'Wow! What a dynamic city! Something special is going on here.'

In Babylon there was so much to inspire awe in the onlooker: temples restored to their former glory; the resplendent blue Ishtar Gate, one of the eight entrance gates to the city; the forty-mile long double or triple fortified wall around the city; and the Hanging Gardens of Babylon, one

26. Mere Christianity by CS Lewis © copyright CS Lewis Pte 1942, 1943, 1944, 1952. Used with permission.

of the Seven Wonders of the ancient world.[27] As the king gazed on all this magnificence, he could not help musing to himself, 'Is not this the great Babylon *I* have built as the royal residence, by *my* mighty power and for the glory of *my* majesty?' (4:29-30).

Even as the words were still on his lips, a voice came from heaven: '"This is what is decreed for you, King Nebuchadnezzar: your royal authority has been taken from you. You will be driven away from people and will live with the wild animals; you will eat grass like the ox. ..." Immediately what had been said about Nebuchadnezzar was fulfilled' (4:31-33).

Why did judgement fall so suddenly upon Nebuchadnezzar, when he had harboured pride for so long? Why are there people who continue in their pride, apparently unchecked, for many years? And, if we are honest, how have we been able to shelter pride in our hearts without being judged by God? Once again, it is the mystery of God's timing. 'The Lord is not slow in keeping his promise [including the promise that "Pride goes before destruction" – Proverbs 16:18], as some understand slowness. Instead he is patient with you, not wanting anyone to perish, but everyone to come to repentance' (2 Peter 3:9).

Nebuchadnezzar had received a clear warning. God in his wisdom decided that twelve months was sufficient time for him to repent. In the absence of any movement in that direction, God carried out his threat.

---

27. The Ishtar Gate stood 48ft (15m) tall and 86ft (26m) wide. Its walls were decorated with glazed bricks which formed raised reliefs of dragons, lions, and bulls set on a brilliant blue background. The bricks were excavated between 1899 and 1917, then shipped to Berlin, where they were cleaned, restored, and reassembled in the Pergamon Museum, where it can be seen today.

It is reckoned that Nebuchadnezzar used 15 million bricks for his various building projects. See https://biblearchaeologyreport.com/2019/10/17/nebuchadnezzar-an-archaeological-biography/.

Whether the Hanging Gardens were in Babylon, or whether they existed at all, is still being disputed by historians. But the tradition which has given them the name by which they are universally known leaves Babylon as their most likely location.

The king 'was driven away from people and ate grass like the ox'. So repulsive did he become that 'His body was drenched with the dew of heaven until his hair grew like the feathers of an eagle and his nails like the claws of a bird' (4:33).

Reflection:

When have I experienced pride coming before a fall, in myself or in others? What have I learned from these experiences?

Why is it, as C.S. Lewis says, so easy to see pride in the hearts of other people and so difficult to see it in myself?

Who would I be willing to ask if they see any pride or arrogance in my own heart?

Am I willing to ask God if there are any words that I have received from him in the past that I have allowed to slip out of my consciousness?

Grace

Nebuchadnezzar was probably not the first monarch who went insane, and he was certainly not the last. The Roman empire had Caligula, who made his horse a consul. Fourteenth-century France was ruled by Charles le Fou (Charles VI, the Crazy), who in his increasingly frequent and longer bouts of insanity believed he was made of glass, attacked servants and ran until exhaustion, wailing that he was being threatened by his enemies. Portugal in the eighteenth century had Maria a Louca (Maria the Mad), who would lie in her apartments all day, her terrible screams echoing through the palace. Britain's George III (who reigned

1760-1820) suffered from increasingly severe rage attacks, panic attacks, delusions and visual and auditory hallucinations as he became older. These are just a few.

Nebuchadnezzar stands apart from all those monarchs. Their condition deteriorated as they grew older, and they never recovered their sanity. In contrast, Nebuchadnezzar did recover his, and he never fell into insanity again. What made the difference? The grace of God. The word 'grace' does not appear in the book of Daniel, and is much less common in the Old Testament than in the New. However, the definition of grace is 'unmerited favour'; and that is exactly what Nebuchadnezzar received from God.

The Bible shows us just how powerfully grace operates through the example of Saul. He was an ardent Pharisee – a member of the strictest Jewish religious group – whose life mission was to maintain the purity of Judaism by persecuting and destroying the infant Church wherever he could find it. In the normal run of things, he would have carried on doing that until the day he died. But his life took a very different turn.

Writing under his new name, Paul, he tells us, '*The grace of our Lord* was poured out on me abundantly, along with the faith and love that are in Christ Jesus' (1 Timothy 1:14). 'I am the least of the apostles and do not even deserve to be called an apostle, because I persecuted the church of God. But *by the grace of God* I am what I am, and his grace to me was not without effect' (1 Corinthians 15:9-10). Grace transformed him. The persecuting Pharisee became one of the leading figures in the first generation of the Church.

Grace can turn our failures into opportunities for growth. A friend told me about one of his young colleagues who made a bad decision that cost his company £10 million. Pressure was put on the young man's boss to dismiss him. But he replied, 'I've just invested £10 million in this young man's personal development and training. I'm not about to let him go.' The boss knew that he would never make that same mistake again, and he would be the wiser for it.

It is said that one of the reasons that E.J. Smith was chosen as captain of the fateful ship *Titanic* was his boast, 'In all my experience, I have never been in any accident ... or any sort worth speaking about. I have seen but one vessel in distress in all my years at sea. I never saw a wreck and never have been wrecked nor was I ever in any predicament that threatened to end in disaster of any sort.'[28] So, when disaster loomed, he had no experience to call upon that would have guided him in how to act. It may have been wiser to have appointed a captain who had survived a shipwreck.

'Though the righteous fall seven times, they rise again' (Proverbs 24:16). We who follow Christ Jesus are righteous not because we are especially good, but because we have accepted *his* righteousness, which is far superior to any of our own. Yet, even then, Proverbs tells us, it is likely that we will fall. However, we will get up again; and our character will have been developed as a result.

We saw just now how quickly the apostle Peter's bravado turned into flat denials that he even knew Jesus. Later on that fateful day, while Jesus was dying on the cross, Peter was nowhere to be seen. Obviously (according to human logic), after such an abject failure at such a critical juncture, Peter was no longer fit to be the leader of the disciples. But grace defies human logic.

After Jesus had risen from the dead, he approaches Peter with his grace and restores him (see John 21:15-19). Peter went on to become the foremost apostle to the Jews (see Galatians 2:8). And he remembers the grace he received, to his dying day. In his two short letters in the New Testament the Greek word *charis,* usually translated 'grace', appears no fewer than twelve times.

---

28. See, for example, http://www.quotationspage.com/quote/22207.html.

Grace is not reserved only for 'spiritual giants' like Paul or Peter or for important people like Nebuchadnezzar. '*To each one of us* grace has been given as Christ apportioned it' (Ephesians 4:7). It is freely available to every single person. There is no failure or sin that could cause God to refuse us his grace, if we approach him in humility.

One of the most staggering examples of this is found in the Old Testament, in the story of Ahab. 'There was never anyone like Ahab, who sold himself to do evil in the eyes of the LORD, urged on by Jezebel his wife' (1 Kings 21:25). He was desperate to extend his palace by buying up some land from his neighbour Naboth; but Naboth would not sell to him. So he had him put to death on trumped-up charges. Then, as he was going down to take possession of his ill-gotten land, the Lord sent the prophet Elijah to meet him and pronounce severe judgement on him (see 1 Kings 21:16-24).

How did Ahab react to this? 'When Ahab heard these words, he tore his clothes, put on sackcloth and fasted. He lay in sackcloth and went around meekly' (1 Kings 21:27). And what was God's response? 'The word of the LORD came to Elijah the Tishbite: "Have you noticed how Ahab has humbled himself before me? Because he has humbled himself, I will not bring this disaster in his day"' (1 Kings 21:28-29).

Now that is Amazing Grace! And the man who penned the hymn of that name knew what he was writing about. Before becoming an Anglican minister, for many years John Newton was the captain of slave ships and an investor in the slave trade. Nobody is too bad to be outside the reach of God's grace.

If you review your own faith story, it is very likely that you will discover, like me, that the grace of God was shown to you before you responded to him. God loved us before we ever loved him (see 1 John 4:10). That is how it was with Nebuchadnezzar too. In his dream the angelic messenger calls out, 'Let the stump and its roots, bound with iron and bronze, remain in the ground, in the grass of the field' (4:15). Daniel interprets this for the king, 'The command to leave the stump of the tree with its roots means that your kingdom will be restored to you when you acknowledge that Heaven rules' (4:26). Restoration is promised to the king before he has even had time to consider the dream.

When I moved into my present house, I found an unwanted young ash tree which had set itself in the middle of a rhododendron bush. I cut down the tree, which was by that time about 7ft (2m) tall, but within a few weeks I found a number of shoots growing vigorously out of the stump. My nurseryman told me, the ash and the sycamore are the thugs of the garden; they will take over if allowed to. New life spontaneously appeared from the stump of the ash tree, and I could only stop it by repeated applications of poison.

What wonderful grace of God towards Nebuchadnezzar! Even though he knew that the king was not going to respond quickly to the warnings of the dream, he still offers him hope for the future. The stump of the tree is to be left in the ground so that new shoots can grow from it one day. And those new shoots will be different.

In one of the houses that I lived in, I could see in a neighbour's garden a 30ft (9m)-high sycamore growing from the stump of a tree that had been cut down. Despite its height, it had an inherent fragility because the base of its trunk was not vertical but came out of the stump at an angle. We were always concerned that it might blow over in a gale, but thankfully it never did while we lived there. Although Nebuchadnezzar was to become 'even greater than before' (4:36), like that sycamore tree, he would have an inherent fragility, which would lead him to recognise his dependence on the Most High.

The grace of God gave the king a whole twelve months to respond to the dream. Even in his insanity, grace continued to be poured out on him. For, somehow, he was enabled to 'raise his eyes towards heaven' and recover his sanity (4:34). He finally took hold of the opportunity that grace offered him. For grace, like eternal life, needs to be taken hold of (see 1 Timothy 6:12). 'The grace of God has appeared that offers salvation to all people. It teaches us to say "No" to ungodliness and worldly passions, and to live self-controlled, upright and godly lives in this present age' (Titus 2:11-12).

Reflection:

What experience do I have of receiving grace from God? Can I recall a particular occasion when I received his grace after having fallen into a sin or having made a serious mistake?

How has the experience of receiving grace shaped my view of God? How has it helped me to show grace to other people?

Is there somebody I know who needs to receive God's grace? How might I encourage them to take hold of it, perhaps citing the example of my own experience?

CHAPTER 5
RECOVERY
(DANIEL 4:34-37)

One small step for man

How did Nebuchadnezzar take hold of the grace that was offered to him? He took one simple step: He 'raised his eyes towards heaven' (4:34). It was, as Neil Armstrong famously said as he put the first ever human foot on the surface of the moon, 'One small step for man, one giant leap for mankind.' For the decision of this one man would affect the whole of the Babylonian Empire.

Nebuchadnezzar's experience is a good illustration of the apostle James' encouragement, 'Come near to God and he will come near to you' (James 4:8). The king took one small step towards God, then God in return took a massive step towards him. Yet, so often we are hesitant to come near to God. We may have a nagging voice telling us that we are not worthy. Or we may be reminded of some shameful thing from our past. Or we may fear that God's primary aim in coming near to us is to find fault with us or convict us of some sin. We may even think that he has lost interest in us. These are all lies. When we resist the lies and take a faltering step towards him, he takes a much bigger step towards us.

I realise now that this was a key element in the process that led to me first meeting Jesus. For months I had been searching in all kinds of places for something that was true and supernatural, something I could commit myself to. I was pretty sure that Christianity was not this something, based on my childhood experience of rather dead churches. But I thought I at least ought to read the New Testament, so that I could say why it was not true from a more informed position. I read it from cover to cover, making notes about all the things that I considered to be wrong or inconsistent. Two months later God broke into my life and introduced me to Jesus Christ. In reading the New Testament, I had taken a small step towards him, even though it was a step based on very questionable motives. He took a massive step towards me.

Watchman Nee was a well-known Chinese church leader of the twentieth century who was targeted by the Chinese Communist Party when they came to power and spent the last twenty years of his life in prison. Whenever he was called to give counsel to a person, he invited them to pray, whether or not they were a Christian. If they said they were an atheist, he would suggest to them that if there really was no God, they would not lose a great deal by speaking words into the air. So, why not pray? He knew that the act of praying was a drawing near to God, and that God in turn would draw near to that person.

When I am mentoring or praying for Christians, I often encourage them to pray out loud, because when they express their heart to God in this way, it creates a dynamic of openness towards him. But I must admit, I have rarely followed Watchman Nee's example and encouraged those who are not Christians to speak out a prayer and take that step towards God.

If we do take a step towards God and he comes near to us, we will quickly be faced with the need to humble ourselves before him – and the prospect of this may well put us off. I did not read the New Testament in an attitude of humility – far from it! But once God had broken into my life, he made clear to me that, if I wanted to continue to enjoy his new life, I had to choose to go his way. For me that was deeply humbling, because I had always prided myself on being master of my own decisions, on me being the one who chose my way in life – although in reality I was nowhere near as autonomous as I imagined. Grace is given to the humble (see James 4:6).

C.S. Lewis has a very perceptive observation: 'A proud man is always looking down on things and people; and, of course, as long as you are looking down, you cannot see something that is above you.'[29] Before his insanity, Nebuchadnezzar was constantly looking down: at courtiers who were subservient or obsequious towards him; at conquered peoples who were subject to him; at the marvellous city of Babylon which was all his own making, so he thought. For somebody who had been accustomed to looking down, 'raising his eyes towards heaven' (4:34), acknowledging that there was a power in the universe far greater than him, was a massive step of humility.

When he raised his eyes, Nebuchadnezzar realised that the Most High has an 'eternal dominion' (4:34) which is superior even to the one which he had been ruling over. He had already been warned in his earlier dream (see Daniel 2) that one day that kingdom would come to an end. Now he recognises that there is only one kingdom, the kingdom of the Most High, that 'endures from generation to generation'. He realises that 'All the peoples of the earth are regarded as nothing. The Most High does as he pleases', not only with 'the peoples of the earth' but also with 'the powers of heaven'. 'No one can hold back his hand or say to him, "What have you done?"' (4:34-35).

When Daniel interpreted the king's earlier dream of the great statue, Nebuchadnezzar was very grateful and declared to Daniel – but not directly to God – 'Surely your God is the God of gods and the Lord of kings and a revealer of mysteries' (2:47). At that time God was still remote to him, and there was no real heart change. Here it is completely

29. Mere Christianity by CS Lewis © copyright CS Lewis Pte 1942, 1943, 1944, 1952. Used with permission.

different. The king praises, honours and glorifies God directly (see 4:34), from a place of humility. His heart has been changed.

Reflection:

When I want to come near to God, do I ever find that I 'have the desire to do what is good, but ... cannot carry it out' (Romans 7:18)? How could I discover what is hindering me from doing what I would like to do?

What experience have I had of humbling myself (or being humbled) in order to receive God's grace? What might hinder me from humbling myself now?

Is there somebody who is not yet following Jesus whom I could encourage in some way to come near to God?

Breaking

For Nebuchadnezzar to reach that place of humility, there needed to be a breaking, just as there needed to be a breaking within me when I first met Jesus. I was struggling to sleep, struggling even to concentrate on my work, losing confidence in myself, desperately looking for solutions but not finding any. My desperation broke my pride and enabled me to respond to God in humility.

Breaking experiences are rarely once and for all. Some will be very dramatic, like at my conversion, and like here with Nebuchadnezzar; others will be much less so. Many of you will be able to identify a time which was intensely difficult, even dark, when you wondered whether you would manage to get through to the other side. One of my hardest times was around twenty-five years ago when I felt a flood of difficulties and criticism coming at me in the church that I was leading. I remember saying to my wife, 'It feels as if something is trying to destroy me as a person.'

By the grace of God, I survived, with the support of my leadership team. Looking back, if you ask me whether I would like to go through an experience like that again, my answer would be a resounding, 'No!' However, if you ask me whether I regret having gone through that experience, the unhesitating answer would also be, 'No!' For I know that when I came out of it, through to the other side, something had radically changed inside me; and other people perceived it too.

Breaking experiences are fraught with potential danger. Some people are like Humpty Dumpty in the nursery rhyme: 'All the king's horses and all the king's men [not even those of King Jesus], Couldn't put Humpty together again.' Some people are destroyed by the breaking. Others remain broken for many years. Some never recover. There is no formula for getting through to the other side without being destroyed. The things which I have found most useful have been: hanging on to God; maintaining my habitual spiritual exercises each day; being part of a Christian community, and having good, supportive friends and a good, supportive wife to help me along the way.

The apostle Peter knew plenty about suffering, and he tells us, 'Whoever suffers in the body has finished with sin' (1 Peter 4:1). That is a hard verse to interpret, but I see it reflected in a small way in my own experience. I know that during that very difficult time something unholy within me broke. Part of that something was pride and self-reliance, although before the breaking I would not have recognised their presence in my life. It is, then, no surprise that the Lord says, 'I live in a high and holy place, but also with the one who is contrite and lowly in spirit, to revive the spirit of the lowly and to revive the heart of the contrite' (Isaiah 57:15). The Hebrew word translated 'contrite' literally means 'crushed'. It is hard to embrace being crushed in spirit, but the rewards are great.

This breaking, crushing process was at work in Nebuchadnezzar, during the 'seven times' of his insanity. It opened him up to the transforming power of God, creating a humility and a dependence on God which are demonstrable in the last few verses of Daniel 4. We know nothing of Nebuchadnezzar's life after the restoration of his sanity, except that he remained a military campaigner, constantly seeking to expand his empire by conquest. For empires have a natural urge to expand, just as in Ezekiel 31 the Assyrian Empire is represented by a massive cedar tree, which seeks constantly to grow and spread itself out.

However, after the experience of being broken, I suspect that Nebuchadnezzar's character would have changed and he would have been a better, more compassionate ruler. His courtiers would have noticed a difference, and the word would quickly have spread abroad. For example, his fits of rage, such as when Shadrach, Meshach and Abednego refused to comply with his orders (see 3:19-23), quite probably became less frequent and less intense. Maybe they disappeared altogether. I certainly found that one transformational effect from my time of breaking was that the anger inside of me considerably shrunk.

Reflection:

Can I identify an experience where I felt that I was being broken? To what extent did external factors contribute to the experience? To what extent did my own attitude of heart contribute (looking back with the benefit of hindsight)?

What helped me to get through to the other side of that experience?

What changes did it bring about in me? To what extent have I sensed a greater openness to God and his Spirit as a result of it?

How could I help somebody who is going through a breaking experience?

Restoration and honour

'Before a downfall the heart is haughty, but humility comes before honour', says Solomon (Proverbs 18:12). Nebuchadnezzar responded to God in humility, and history remembers him, not as the megalomaniac king who went mad – indeed, many historians do not even accept the historicity of his episode of insanity. Rather, he is recalled as the greatest ruler of the Babylonian Empire, the one who brought it to its zenith – honour indeed!

That is the macro-narrative of the apostle Peter's life too. After his denial of Jesus, he responded with humility, and he is honoured in the Bible as the premier apostle to the Jews (see Galatians 2:8); and tradition honours him as the first bishop of Rome. King David humbled himself at the prophet Nathan's rebuke (see 2 Samuel 12), after having committed adultery and murder; and he is now remembered as the greatest ever king of Israel. Even Jesus honours him by accepting for himself the title 'Son of David'.

In 1963 the British establishment was rocked by the Profumo affair, and it is reckoned to have contributed substantially to the fall of the Conservative government the following year. John Profumo, Minister of War and a potential future prime minister, had a sexual relationship with Christine Keeler, thirty years younger than him. She was also sleeping with an attaché at the Soviet embassy – and this was at the height of the Cold War. Profumo lied about the affair to his wife, to his friends and to parliament. When the truth finally came out, he was obliged to resign in disgrace.

Profumo then humbled himself, spending forty years working with the poor at Toynbee Hall in the East End of London. Honour came to him with the award of the CBE in 1975. Then, when he died in 2006, he was honoured by no less than the prime minister, Tony Blair: 'I think he will be remembered not just for the events that brought his political career to an end, but also he will be remembered with a lot of gratitude and respect for what he achieved in his later life. It must have been very difficult to do it, but he did do it.'[30] Three years earlier, his longstanding friend, Bill Deedes, met him at Toynbee Hall and asked him what he had learned from working there. He replied with one word, 'Humility.'[31] For John Profumo too, humility came before honour.

Along with Nebuchadnezzar's recovery came restoration. He tells us, 'At the same time that my sanity was restored, my honour and splendour were returned to me for the glory of my kingdom. My advisors and nobles sought me out and I was restored to my throne and became even greater than before' (4:36). Like the king, Peter was also restored to a position of leadership, in his case in the early Church. However, it does not always happen like that. John Profumo was restored, but never held political office again. His new role was a more humble one, though perhaps a more useful one.

The good news of Jesus Christ is that our heavenly Father is a God of restoration. When we mess up, it is never beyond redemption, if we are willing to come near to God in humility. We may or may not recover the position which we had before. We may well bear the scars of our past mistakes and misdeeds for the rest of our life, just as one of my good friends all his life bore the scars of injecting himself with drugs

30. https://www.nytimes.com/2006/03/11/obituaries/john-profumo-91-former-british-minister-caught-in-sex-scandal.html.

31. https://www.telegraph.co.uk/culture/3606783/What-Profumo-did-next.html.

before he had come to know Jesus. But those very scars may keep us humble and make us a more effective friend and servant of our Lord Jesus. The apostle Paul warns, 'Let no one cause me trouble, for I bear on my body the marks of Jesus' (Galatians 6:17) – the scars of being violently assaulted in persecution, certainly; but perhaps also the scars from his earlier life, which Jesus allowed to remain there and to which he alludes in 1 Corinthians 15:8-10.

Nebuchadnezzar was not only restored to his throne, but he 'became even greater than before' (4:36). That is how our God restores: not grudgingly or sparingly, for he 'gives generously to all without finding fault' (James 1:5). Therefore, Peter was not only restored to being the leader of a group of twelve disciples, but became a key leader of a Church which turned the world upside down. David was not only restored as king, but was allowed to set in motion the preparations for building a temple for the Lord. He established a dynasty that lasted 400 years and which led directly to the birth of the Messiah.

Jonathan Aitken's story did not end with prison and bankruptcy. Like John Profumo, he was not restored to parliament or to political office; so he never did become prime minister. But he found restoration in the grace of Jesus Christ and in the humility to receive that grace. Since his release from prison in 1998 he has studied theology, written books, been extensively involved in prison reform and prisoner rehabilitation, and has been ordained as a Church of England minister. The BBC's religion editor wrote after interviewing him: 'The disgraced former MP says he was liberated while serving a prison sentence for perjury eighteen years ago; bankrupted yet found something beyond earthly treasure; was reduced to the depths but raised to the heights. It doesn't seem to make sense.'[32]

32. https://www.radiotimes.com/news/tv/2018-08-14/faith-behind-bars-former-tory-mp-jonathan-aitken-interview/.

The grace of God never makes sense to our human logic. 'Where sin increased, grace increased all the more' (Romans 5:20). Trouble may come to us through our own sin, through the sin of other people, or simply through living in a sinful world. God's grace does not merely counteract the trouble, however great it may be, but he gives a double blessing in its place. Paul persecuted the Church, but became one of its principal architects. Peter denied Jesus, but grace enabled him to spend the rest of his days boldly proclaiming him.

At one time Nebuchadnezzar was full of his own self-importance, but God's grace made him greater than ever, and enabled him to confess, 'I praise and exalt and glorify the King of heaven, because everything he does is right and all his ways are just. And those who walk in pride he is able to humble' (4:37). The king remembers where he has come from, and he has no intention of going back there.

One final reflection on Daniel 4: Was King Nebuchadnezzar really converted? Did he become a true believer and live in a different way? Or did he fall back again into his old idolatrous ways after this experience? Does the awful prophecy against the king of Babylon in Isaiah 14 apply to him personally?

In the final resort we have to say that we do not know for sure. We know very little of the final thirty years of his reign, other than what is in the biblical record. Jeremiah (43:8-13) and Ezekiel (29:17 - 30:26) prophesied that he would invade and destroy Egypt, but we cannot be sure when that was (see Appendix C). Even that invasion was in line with God's purposes, according to the prophecy of Ezekiel. And we know nothing of Nebuchadnezzar's heart and mind in that thirty-year period.

What we do know is that the events of this chapter became well known throughout the Babylonian court. Twenty-three years after his death, when Babylon was in danger of being overrun by the Medes and Persians, King Belshazzar calls for Daniel to interpret some mysterious handwriting which has appeared on the wall of his palace (see 5:10-16). Daniel recounts to him the whole story of Nebuchadnezzar's insanity, humbling and restoration (see 5:18-21). Then he turns to the king and says, 'But you, Belshazzar, his son, have not humbled yourself, *though you knew all this*' (5:22-23). So it seems most likely that Nebuchadnezzar did not go back on the steps which he took towards God.

There is a principle which I have found very helpful in interpreting Scripture and which will be of assistance here: In the absence of evidence, always think the best of people or situations. 'Love does not delight in evil. ... It always ... hopes' (1 Corinthians 13:6-7).

The final verses of Daniel 4 and the prophecies of Ezekiel 29:18-19 and 30:10 are the final appearances of Nebuchadnezzar in the Bible, and they contain not a single word of criticism against him. So, in the absence of anything negative, I am content to assume that Nebuchadnezzar continued on the path which he began in this chapter.

My expectation, therefore, is that, when we stand before the throne of our Lord Jesus Christ in that wonderful final day, Nebuchadnezzar will be there among that glorious throng of people – probably not at the head of the group, as he was in his lifetime; but one of the many 'redeemed ... with the precious blood of Christ' (1 Peter 1:18-19). Daniel's faithfulness to him will be seen to have borne fruit.

Will what the king built up in his life survive the testing of fire, or will it be burned up so that he suffers 'loss but yet will be saved – even though only as one escaping through the flames' (1 Corinthians 3:14-15)? None of us can say. In the age to come, 'Many who are first will be last, and many who are last will be first' (Matthew 19:30). There will be many surprises on that day, and I strongly suspect that Nebuchadnezzar will be one of them.

Reflection:

What experience have I had of receiving honour as a result of humbling myself? How did my humbling prepare me to receive the honour?

Can I identify other people who have had this same experience? What can I learn from them?

Do I know of somebody whose career has fallen on hard times or who has been publicly disgraced? If I know them personally, would I be willing to help them? Otherwise, would I be willing to commit to praying for them to turn to God in humility and so receive restoration?

DANIEL 5
THE WILDERNESS

Introduction to Daniel 5

We know exactly when the events of this chapter took place, because historical sources tell us that Babylon was captured in October, 539BC. Somewhere between forty and fifty years have elapsed since the end of Daniel 4 (see Appendix C). Nebuchadnezzar has died and three other kings have come and gone, each of them murdered. A fourth king, Nabonidus, is on the throne, but he spends most of his time away from Babylon and leaves affairs of state in the hands of his son Belshazzar. Daniel by now has been living in Babylon for more than sixty-five years and is a very old man (in those days of reduced life expectancy), at least in his late seventies.

Although they are decades apart, Daniel 4 and 5 sit well together. Both are centred on God's judgement. Yet there is a stark contrast in the way in which the kings in each chapter responded to that judgement. Nebuchadnezzar repented and is remembered as perhaps the greatest of the Babylonian kings. Belshazzar, in this chapter, had gone beyond repentance, and is remembered only as the Babylonian king who convened a glorious feast and was then conquered and killed by the Medes and Persians.

Once again, the plot of this chapter is simple. King Belshazzar holds a massive feast for his nobles, and while they are in a state of high intoxication he decides to bring in the vessels of the temple of the Lord which Nebuchadnezzar had captured from Jerusalem many years earlier. While they are all drinking from them and praising pagan gods, a disembodied hand appears and writes a mysterious message on the wall of the room. The king is terrified and nobody is able to interpret the writing. Then the queen mother remembers Daniel from the distant past. He is brought in and, faithful as ever to God, he is able to explain to the king that the writing foretells his death and the end of the Babylonian Empire at the hand of the Medes and Persians. Those things then come to pass, that very same night.

Over the centuries a host of composers, playwrights, authors, poets and painters have taken inspiration from Belshazzar's feast. Yet many scholars still dispute the historical accuracy of the events of Daniel 5. They have five principal objections.

Firstly, they say that this chapter presents Belshazzar as a king, but he was not. Nabonidus was indeed king of Babylon at that time, but we know that during his long absences from Babylon he left his son in charge, so that Belshazzar exercised the functions of a regent, a kind of 'acting king' – just as George IV of Britain was regent from 1811 to 1820, when his father, George III, became increasingly mentally unstable. It is therefore entirely reasonable to refer to Belshazzar as 'king'. In fact, the Bible recognises that he was not the overall ruler of Babylon. For he is only able to offer to the successful interpreter of the writing on the wall the position of *third* highest ruler in the kingdom (see 5:7) – he being the second and his father the first.

The second objection is that Nebuchadnezzar is referred to as the father of Belshazzar, whereas Belshazzar was the biological son of Nabonidus. Some scholars suggest that he married a daughter of Nebuchadnezzar called Nitocris, in which case Nebuchadnezzar would be his father-in-law; but this cannot be substantiated. The Nabonidus Chronicle, an ancient Babylonian text inscribed on clay tablets, describes Belshazzar as a grandson of Nebuchadnezzar, which may well have been propaganda to give him credibility because he was not of the royal line.

So, these references to Nebuchadnezzar as Belshazzar's 'father' may simply reflect the court propaganda of the time. It is noteworthy that when Daniel speaks of 'your father Nebuchadnezzar' (5:18), and when he points to the king, 'But you, Belshazzar, his son ...' (5:22), not one person of all those present stands up and says, 'Hang on, Daniel. You've got that wrong.' They all accepted the accuracy of what he was saying.

Even today, we often use the term 'father' in a much broader sense than 'biological parent'. We speak, for example, of Hippocrates as 'the father of modern medicine', of Ernest Rutherford as 'the father of nuclear physics'. So, Aramaic and Hebrew, which are much more flexible than our Western languages, allow for 'your father Nebuchadnezzar' to mean simply 'your illustrious predecessor, the founder of modern Babylon'.

The third objection is that this feast is not mentioned in any other historical source. The other two refer to the final verse of Daniel 5: it is said that the Persians alone conquered Babylon, and not the Medes and Persians; and that Darius the Mede is a purely fictitious character. I will deal with these points in Chapter 10, when we come to Daniel 6.

Reflection:

Read Daniel 5. What title would I give to this chapter (other than the obvious *Belshazzar's Feast*)? If I was directing it as a film, who would I cast in the roles of Belshazzar and Daniel?

Why should I have confidence in the biblical record when it is not backed up by other historical sources?

CHAPTER 6
DUTCH COURAGE
(DANIEL 5:1-9)

(False) confidence boosting

We can read today about rich people throwing lavish parties for hundreds of guests to celebrate their birthday or their child's wedding. Then there are official banquets which a monarch gives to a visiting head of state and which last only one evening. Belshazzar's feast was way in excess of these, in terms of both extravagance and duration: more than 1,000 illustrious guests (see 5:1); probably lasting many days; and quite riotous (see 5:2-4).

We know quite a lot about feasting in the ancient Near East. For example:

> Feasts are opulent events – a sumptuous, vibrant display of lavish quantities of highly valued, possibly otherwise restricted, food and drink, which the host shares out amongst the participants in a feast of extravagant consumption. ... Individuals are able to gain prestige and status from their largesse and perceived generosity, whilst at the same time binding their guests to them in a network of obligation and reciprocity. The hospitality of the feast is used to forge political, military and dynastic alliances, against a backdrop

of conviviality, gift exchanges, entertainment and display.[33]

Belshazzar's feast fits this description very well. Back in February 2022 our television screens were filled with images of 150,000 Russian troops massing on the Ukraine border, ready to pounce at any time. That is how it was for Babylon on this fateful day. The massed troops of the Medes and Persians had reached to within a few miles of the gates of Babylon.

The king urgently needed to firm up his rule. He needed friends whom he could rely on in a crisis. He needed to demonstrate that he was the strong man in the city, the one whom people should stick by. He needed to show that loyalty to him would be richly rewarded. Through the lavishness of his hospitality, Belshazzar sought to strengthen his alliances with key players and render them indebted to him. The feast would also have been a welcome diversion from the constant worries about a possible invasion.

Belshazzar had thrown a very big party: 1,000 nobles, not including their wives and concubines – all getting very drunk, very merry and very bold (see 5:1-4). Yet even this feast pales into insignificance when compared with other ancient Near Eastern celebrations. For example, in 879BC Ashurnasirpal II, king of Assyria, invited his whole country to a festival to celebrate the completion of his new city, Kalhu. Seventy thousand people turned up.

Belshazzar's feast was crucial to him keeping his hands on the reins of power. However, things reached such a point that he began to worry that the feasting was not proving to be enough of a distraction from the invasion threat. Something was needed to bolster the confidence of his guests. What better than bringing into the room articles which

33. Louise Steel, 'Sumptuous Feasting in the Ancient Near East: Exploring the Materiality of the Royal Tombs of Ur' in Louise Steel, Katharina Zinn, eds, *Exploring the Materiality of Food 'Stuffs': Transformations, symbolic consumptions and embodiments,* Routledge Series in Archaeology (New York: Routledge, 2019), pp. 189-204.

recalled past glories and which tangibly demonstrated the power of the Babylonian gods against all others? So, fired up by alcohol-fuelled courage (which the English call 'Dutch courage'[34]), he ordered, 'Bring in the gold and silver goblets that King Nebuchadnezzar took from the temple in Jerusalem!' (see 5:2).

This command was not a random whim, the sort of thing that people are prone to do when they are drunk. Through the centuries the Lord the God of Israel had acquired a reputation for himself in the Middle East. People of many nations remembered how he had done the impossible and set free his people, a dispirited, rag-tag group of slaves, from Egypt, the superpower of the day.

The impact of this deliverance lasted a long time. Two hundred years afterwards, when the Israelites in desperation brought the ark of the Lord (representing his presence) into battle, their Philistine adversaries were terrified. '"A god has come into the camp," they said. "Oh no! Nothing like this has happened before. We're doomed! Who will deliver us from the hand of these mighty gods? They are the gods who struck the Egyptians with all kinds of plagues in the wilderness"' (1 Samuel 4:7-8).

The Lord's reputation continued to spread. Three hundred years before the events of this chapter, King Jeshoshaphat won a spectacular military victory through the direct intervention of the Lord, and 'the fear of God came on all the surrounding kingdoms when they heard how the LORD had fought against the enemies of Israel' (2 Chronicles 20:29).

The Babylonians would also have known how, 150 years earlier, the tiny kingdom of Judah under King Hezekiah had been the only one in

34. There is no general agreement on how this expression was coined. The best explanations that I have found are that English soldiers drank jenever (a type of Dutch gin) before a battle to counter fear; or that they saw Dutch soldiers drinking jenever and witnessed the bravery with which they fought after it.

the region to hold out against the might of the Assyrian Empire, and how the Lord had put to death 185,000 Assyrian soldiers in one night, sending the mighty King Sennacherib packing, back to Nineveh and to his death (see Isaiah 37).

Even many years *after* the events of Daniel 5, despite the destruction of Jerusalem, the reputation of the Lord had not dwindled. The Persian king Artaxerxes discovered, 'Jerusalem has had powerful kings ruling over the whole of Trans-Euphrates, and taxes, tribute and duty were paid to them' (Ezra 4:20). In those days the strength of a kingdom directly reflected the strength of its gods. So this God of Israel was not to be messed with!

Today most people in the West no longer believe in the power of gods to influence a nation's destiny. Yet many still judge God's reputation on what they see in the place where his kingdom is being expressed today, namely the Church. For example, the atheist philosopher Bertrand Russell, in addition to his philosophical objections to religion, stated, 'I say quite deliberately that the Christian religion, as organised in its Churches, has been and still is the principal enemy of moral progress in the world.'[35] Those with less philosophical education say, 'There are so many hypocrites in the Church. People there are no better than me. So why should I join them?'

Jesus was well aware that this would happen. For, just hours before his death he prays to his Father for all believers: 'May they be brought to complete unity. *Then the world will know* that you sent me and have loved them even as you have loved me' (John 17:23). The New Testament letters are full of exhortations to be aware of how our behaviour is perceived by those outside the Church (e.g. 1 Peter 3:13-16; 1 Timothy 3:7; Colossians 4:5; 1 Thessalonians 4:11-12). The consequences of failing to live up to our calling are sobering, as Paul tells the Jews of

35. Bertrand Russell, *Why I Am Not a Christian* (NY: Simon & Schuster, 1957), p. 21.

his day: 'God's name is blasphemed among the Gentiles because of you' (Romans 2:24).

Belshazzar saw that bringing down the reputation of the Lord, the God of Israel, and exalting the Babylonian gods would be a sure-fire way to inspire confidence in his guests and so strengthen his hold on power – and he needed that! So he calls for a concrete reminder of how Babylon had vanquished the God who even the mighty Assyrians could not stand up to. 'Bring in the gold and silver goblets that King Nebuchadnezzar took from the temple in Jerusalem!' (see 5:2). 'We overcame the Lord, and now we shall desecrate his holy vessels. He will be powerless to do anything about it.'

This seems to have had the desired effect. For, as they drank wine from these vessels, their confidence levels rose. 'They praised the gods of gold and silver, of bronze, iron, wood and stone' (5:4). Their idols, made of gold, silver, bronze, iron, wood or stone, had overcome the most powerful gods in the region. So the Medes and the Persians with their inferior gods would be no problem! Let's not allow them to distract us from our partying!

Reflection:

Where do I see leaders today seeking to inspire confidence in their leadership in the midst of difficult circumstances (in a country, a company, a church ...)? To what extent are their efforts finding success? What can I learn from their success or failure?

How would I assess the reputation in my country of the God and Father of our Lord Jesus Christ? How much of this is based on people's perceptions of the Church?

Mercy and judgement

The new-found confidence of Belshazzar and his guests did not last very long. 'Suddenly the fingers of a human hand appeared and wrote on the plaster of the wall, near the lampstand in the royal palace' (5:5). No wonder that the king's 'face turned pale and he was so frightened that his legs became weak and his knees were knocking' (5:6).

What prompted God to act in such a dramatic way and at that precise moment? We human beings are so often struggling with the question of why God does or does not intervene in particular situations, maybe within our own personal experience, or perhaps in national or global situations. So, it is worth spending some time considering why God does or does not bring his judgement to the earth, looking at examples from the Bible.

First of all, we should admit that we are always going to struggle to understand the timing of a God for whom 'a day is like a thousand years, and a thousand years are like a day' (2 Peter 3:8). Anybody who says, 'I am coming soon' (Revelation 22:20) and has still not come 2,000 years later is going to give us problems with his timing.

I recall a preacher telling of an experience at Speakers' Corner in Hyde Park, London. That is a place where anybody is free to speak on any subject they like, provided that they do not resort to hate speech. An atheist was holding forth passionately about the follies of religion. He paused, then confidently asserted, 'I am now going to prove to you conclusively that God does not exist.' He looked heavenward, shook his fist at the God he believed to be imaginary and challenged him, 'If you exist, then send a thunderbolt down on me, right now!' There was a pregnant pause. Nothing happened. He turned triumphantly to his audience, 'See, there is no God!'

The preacher asked rhetorically how a mortal man could ever think that he could order the Almighty God when and how to send judgement on the earth. How indeed? Every single day, in every single part of the world, acts which deserve God's judgement are being committed more times than can be counted. Yet thankfully, thunderbolts are not constantly raining down from heaven upon us. 'Mercy triumphs over judgment' (James 2:13).

Mercy triumphs over judgement, because the Lord tells us, 'I take no pleasure in the death of the wicked, but rather that they turn from their ways and live' (Ezekiel 33:11). However, mercy does not obliterate judgement. As with Belshazzar here, there comes a point when judgement falls. Why does it delay? What causes it to fall? These are important questions. For, if there is no answer to them, then God may be looked upon as arbitrary, impotent, or even unjust.

Before going into these questions in more depth, it would be good to give ourselves a dose of humility and say, with the apostle Paul, 'Oh the depths of the riches of the wisdom and knowledge of God! How unsearchable his judgments, and his paths beyond tracing out! … For from him and through him and for him are all things' (Romans 11:33,36). We shall never completely understand God's activity, for in this age we only 'know in part' (1 Corinthians 13:9). Yet our God is not totally inscrutable. He graciously allows us to see and understand something of his purposes. So, although we will never reach a definitive resolution of this conundrum, we can confidently look for insights into the issues raised by these questions. Three people from the Bible will help us.

The first person is God's friend, Abraham, the father of all the faithful. When the Lord is choosing him as the founder of a permanent community of faith, he converses with him about the future nation which would be descended from him. He reveals to him that this nation would be enslaved and ill-treated in another country for 400 years. Then he tells him, 'In the fourth generation your descendants will come back here,[36] for the sin of the Amorites [who were occupying the land at that time] has not yet reached its full measure' (Genesis 15:16).

Because God's judgement is always perfectly just, he was only willing to root the Amorites out of their land when he considered that their sin had reached a level that justified such drastic action. Like all the Canaanite nations which Israel dispossessed, the Amorites had many highly cruel and disgusting practices. But God withheld his judgement from them and was not willing for their land to be taken over for at least another 400 years – not even for the sake of Abraham, his friend. Amazing patience!

Fast forward to the present day: every year from 2002 to 2021 North Korea was at the top of the Open Doors World Watch List, as the most dangerous place in the world to be a Christian – Afghanistan took over the 'top spot' in 2022 and pushed North Korea into second place. For more than seventy years the Kim dynasty has brutally, mercilessly and systematically persecuted Christians. Tens of thousands have been executed or have died in appalling misery in labour camps. Even if they manage to flee to China, they are hunted down by North Korean agents. Christians throughout the world have been praying for their North Korean brothers and sisters. Yet, apparently the sin of the Kims has not yet reached its full measure.

It would be good to bear this in mind when we cry out to God for justice, whether for ourselves or for others. We are probably going to have to persist in this prayer. For 'Jesus told his disciples a parable to show them that they should always pray and not give up' (Luke 18:1). He concludes it by saying, 'Will not God bring about justice for his chosen ones, who cry out to him day and night? Will he keep putting them off?

36. There are different views as to what 'In the fourth generation' represents. Some say that at that time a generation was considered as 100 years, so it is simply another way of saying '400 years'. Others say that it is four generations after the end of the 400 years. Whichever interpretation is taken, both represent a very long period of time before 'the sin of the Amorites … reached its full measure'.

I tell you, he will see that they get justice, and quickly' (Luke 18:7-8). We may well need to 'cry out to him day and night'. And God's 'quickly' may not be quite the same as ours.

Reflection:

When have I asked God to bring his judgement into a situation? Did that judgement come? How long did I have to wait for it? Do I have any indication why God delayed (or is still delaying) acting?

Reflecting back, could there have been another more effective request that I could have made to him?

Is there a group or a government that is persecuting Christians and I can pray blessing over them and so 'heap burning coals on their head' (Romans 12:20)?

Judgement, but when?

The second person who will help us in these matters is another Jewish hero: David, the greatest ever king of Israel and Judah. Yet, despite his devotion to the Lord, during his reign there was a famine for three successive years. So he 'sought the face of the LORD' (2 Samuel 21:1). He had the wisdom to know that unusual weather events sometimes have the hand of God behind them.

The answer that came back to him was rather surprising: 'It is on account of Saul and his blood-stained house; it is because he put the Gibeonites to death.' That unwise action of Saul, his predecessor as king, had been a breach of the friendship treaty which the Israelites had made with the Gibeonites many centuries earlier (see Joshua 9). God is not happy when we make a promise or an agreement, then break it.

There is no indication of the time lag between Saul killing the Gibeonites and the famine coming upon the land, but the text implies that it was many years. Judgement had hung over the land like a cloud for all those years because of the shedding of innocent blood. Then suddenly it fell, in the form of a famine. Why it fell at that particular time, when a righteous king was ruling, we are not told. Perhaps it was because only a righteous king would have sought the Lord as David did. Having received an answer from him, he was quick to deal with this unresolved situation from the past, though in a way that seems barbaric to us today. 'After that, God answered prayer on behalf of the land' (2 Samuel 21:14).

All Israel would have known that Saul was violating their treaty with the Gibeonites when he put them to death. But nobody seems to have complained or even bothered about it. The human capacity for ignoring or disregarding the obvious should never be underestimated. David himself is attested as 'a man after God's own heart' (Acts 13:22). Yet, without any pang of conscience, he brought another man's wife into his palace to have sex with her, even while she was still getting over her period; then he arranged for the murder of her husband when he found out that she was pregnant by him.

In David's case, mercy triumphed over judgement. God spared his life; but there was a price to pay. The child conceived illicitly died and the prophet Nathan told him, 'The sword shall never depart from your house, because you despised me and took the wife of Uriah the Hittite to be your own' (2 Samuel 12:10). And so it was.

How can we avoid these blind spots? The apostle Paul helps us, speaking of his own experience: 'I strive always to keep my conscience clear before God and man' (Acts 24:16). Keeping our conscience clear does not happen automatically. It requires effort, striving; but it is well worth the effort. A good way to do this is to pray King David's prayer: 'Search me, God, and know my heart; test me and know my anxious thoughts. See if there is any offensive way in me, and lead me in the way everlasting' (Psalm 139:23-24). We do not need to rake around, desperately searching for some hidden sin. That can actually be harmful, like picking at a scab. We need only to open ourselves to God, then leave it to him to point out anything that will take us away from 'the way everlasting'.

The third person who gives us some understanding of God's timing in bringing judgement to the earth is almost diametrically opposite to Abraham and David. He is Manasseh, one of the most wicked kings of Judah. He 'shed so much innocent blood that he filled Jerusalem from end to end' (2 Kings 21:16). Imagine living in a society like that! Every week one of your friends or colleagues would simply disappear. Sometimes the body would turn up, often horribly mutilated. Everybody knew what had happened, but nobody dared ask any questions or make any comment. For it might be your turn next if you spoke out too openly. Incidentally, that is the reality for Christians in some parts of the world: for example, in Taliban-controlled Afghanistan, or in rural zones of Colombia controlled by drug-trafficking armed groups.

Despite his wickedness, Manasseh reigned longer than any other king in Judah and died at the age of sixty-six – quite old for those times. Nearly forty years passed by after his death. It was only during the reign of his great-grandson Jehoiakim that 'The LORD sent … raiders against King Jehoiakim … because of the sins of Manasseh and all he had done, including the shedding of innocent blood. For he had filled Jerusalem with innocent blood, and the LORD was not willing to forgive' (2 Kings 24:2-4).

Judgement had hung over Judah for nearly forty years as the Lord waited patiently for them to repent. Those bands of raiders were a first warning, but it was not heeded. Repentance did not come. The opportunity to be forgiven lapsed, and fifteen years later Jerusalem was destroyed by the Babylonians.

Why did judgement fall at precisely that time? Why did God wait forty years before beginning to act against the wickedness of Manasseh? We cannot exactly say. Presumably it was only then that the sin of Judah had reached its full measure. The Lord was very patient with them, as he had been with the Amorites earlier. As we saw in Chapter 4, the Lord is patient with the human race, 'not wanting anyone to perish, but everyone to come to repentance' (2 Peter 3:9). 'Our Lord's patience means salvation' (2 Peter 3:15).

These three examples may cause us to despair of God ever intervening during our lifetime. 'Why bother praying?' we may ask ourselves. Two passages of Scripture will help us. The first is Psalm 73, where the psalmist laments his own distressing situation and compares himself with the rich, godless people around him who he sees suffering from none of the troubles that are afflicting him. Then comes a turning point. He confesses, 'It troubled me deeply *till I entered the sanctuary of God*; then I understood their final destiny' (vv. 16-17).

Getting alone with God and laying bare before him our complaints and our confusion enables us to see things more from his perspective. We may well not get any more clarity on his timing – the psalmist did not. But we will gain a deeper appreciation of his ways, as the psalmist did in verses 18-28. And we will certainly gain a deeper appreciation of his love for us, for all human beings, and for all his creation.

The second relevant passage is 2 Thessalonians 1. The apostle Paul commends the Thessalonian church: 'Your faith is growing more and more, and the love all of you have for one another is increasing. Therefore, among God's churches we boast about your perseverance and faith in all the persecutions and trials you are enduring' (vv. 3-4). Then he makes the remarkable statement, 'All this is evidence that God's judgment is right' (v. 5). Faithfulness under difficult circumstances such as persecution is a proof that God's judgement will come at the right time (see v. 6). But that judgement may not definitively occur until 'the Lord Jesus is revealed from heaven in blazing fire with his powerful angels' (v. 7).

Paul encourages the Thessalonian Christians to take the same long-term perspective as the writer of Psalm 73. In our Western society we are used to demanding that things happen immediately: instant coffee, ready meals that only require a few minutes in the microwave, the instant response of our smartphone. So, it is particularly difficult to think ourselves into God's long-term time scale, which is far from instant.

Nobody in the Thessalonian church saw persecution of Christians abate in their lifetime; but they died confident that God would certainly intervene at exactly the right time. And he did – 250 years later, with the conversion of the emperor Constantine. Like so many persecuted believers today, the Thessalonians were powerless to change their circumstances, but they had power to change their attitude, power to take a long-term perspective, and power to continue to trust God. So do we today.

Reflection:

Is there a particular situation in my own life, the life of my church, of my nation, or even a global situation which troubles me? Am I willing to bring this situation into the presence of God? Am I ready to make changes in my attitude, if necessary?

What steps can I take to keep my conscience clear before God and before my fellow humans? Is this purely a personal matter for me, or are there other people who I could usefully involve in this?

What steps could I take to gain a more long-term perspective on my own circumstances and those in the world around me? How could this help me in my relationship with God?

Revelation: help!

Even when God's judgement came to Belshazzar, it came with mercy. The handwriting on the wall can be seen as a wake-up call. The king was halted in his tracks by this unusual, spectacular happening. It is as if God was giving him one final opportunity to stop and consider the folly of what he was doing, to reconsider his ways and repent.

My wife and I were friends with a Christian woman who, it turned out, for many years had lived a life of deceit. She had faked serious illnesses, and encouraged Christian friends to serve her, pay attention to her and give her money. I will spare you the details. Finally, the burden of deceit became too great for her to bear and she took her own life – which was doubly tragic because, if only she had come clean with her friends, we would have all forgiven her and accepted her.

Days before her suicide, we visited her and I gave her a passage of Scripture which I felt God had laid on my heart as an encouragement to her. After she had died, I looked back on those verses, and I realised that they were, in fact, a final act of mercy from God, calling her to repent. I had not understood it at the time; that meaning had been hidden from me, because I did not even realise that she needed to repent. But, through those verses from the Bible, God had made one final appeal to her. Sadly, she refused it, and she died.

Belshazzar received this one final appeal from God. But he too refused to repent. All that interested him was finding out the meaning of the words inscribed on the plaster by the unearthly hand. They were written in Aramaic, the everyday language of the court, and they were familiar enough (see 5:25):

Mene, Mene – a variant of Mina, a unit of weight, and therefore of money (a coin being defined by its weight at that time);
Tekel – a variant of Shekel, another unit of weight and money;
Parsin – literally 'halves', referring to half-minas or half-shekels.

It is as if in present-day Britain the hand had written, 'Fiver, Pound, Penny' or in the USA, 'Dollar, Quarter, Dime'. But what on earth was the *meaning* of these familiar units of money which the hand had so deliberately written on the wall?

Have you ever wondered, like me, why God's revelation in the Bible can sometimes be so difficult to comprehend? I am encouraged by the fact that even Peter, the leader of the apostles, found some things that the apostle Paul had written 'hard to understand' (2 Peter 3:16)! Our finite minds will always have some difficulty in comprehending revelation from an infinite God. They are so orientated towards earthly things that there will always be a struggle to understand truth given from the realm of heaven.

Because the king's mind was totally set on earthly things, he could not make head or tail of the words. So, he did what kings did in those days: he sought the help of his inner circle of courtiers. As Nebuchadnezzar had done many years earlier (see 2:2-3), he summoned his enchanters, astrologers and diviners, and offered them a fantastic reward (see 5:7). But not one of them, the wisest, most educated and most discerning men in his kingdom, could make any sense of the words (see 5:8).

God is not deliberately obtuse. He loves to reveal to us things which are important to him, just as we love talking to our friends about things which are important to us. And that shows us the key: understanding of his revelation is based on friendship, which is rooted in relationship. As we seek to deepen our relationship with God, we gain greater understanding of his revelation.

Therefore, Jesus encourages us, 'Seek, and keep on seeking, and you will find' (Matthew 7:7, literally).[37] This confirms the promise of Proverbs 2:3-5: 'If you call out for insight and cry aloud for understanding, and if you look for it as for silver and search for it as for hidden treasure, then you will understand the fear of the LORD and find the knowledge of God.' Mining for silver, getting it out of the ground and processing it, costs around $12 per ounce ($400/kg) and requires a lot of effort. But there is no shortage of companies willing to make the effort for the rewards to be gained from it. Paraphrasing 1 Corinthians 9:25, 'They do it for something purely material that will not last, but we put effort into searching for wisdom and understanding, things that will last for ever.'

Wisdom says, 'My fruit is better than fine gold; what I yield surpasses choice silver' (Proverbs 8:19). There have been dozens of gold rushes in history, all over the world. Some of the best known are those in California in the 1850s and the Klondike in the 1890s. People were prepared to sell up everything, venture into unknown and dangerous territory, and put up with all kind of privations in their search of gold. How much are we prepared to give up in our search of wisdom, which will be of much more value to us?

Gold prospecting was usually more effective when people worked together, or when you had knowledge of what others were doing, even your strongest competitors. Likewise, the search for wisdom and understanding will be more effective if not conducted in isolation. The apostle Paul says, 'What *we* have received is not the spirit of the world, but the Spirit who is from God, so that *we* may understand what God has freely given *us*' (1 Corinthians 2:12). A few verses on, we read, '*We* have the mind of Christ' (1 Corinthians 2:16).

In our individualistic Western societies it is easy to read the 'we' and the 'us' in these verses as 'I' and 'me'. But the promises are given

37. In the original Greek, the present imperative, which is used here (and in the other two commands in this verse), is a command to do something and carry on doing it.

to groups of Christians, and to the body of Christ as a whole. Learning from the body of Christ will enable us to gain a fuller understanding of God's revelation.

If we find some revelation puzzling, even after a lot of searching, a good first step is to ask somebody to help us, or to consult a group of people such as our home group. We can start with our circle of friends, then maybe widen our search within our own denomination or movement. But to gain a fuller understanding of 'the *whole* counsel of God' (Acts 20:27, ESV), we will need to look further afield, especially towards those parts of the body of Christ that we find very different from ourselves, even those parts that we may disagree with.

Belshazzar did not find the understanding that he needed in his immediate circle. Where could he look further afield? Fortunately for him, in that room there was one person who could point him in the right direction. One person (and only one person) had retained a clear recollection of events which had taken place more than thirty years earlier, in marked contrast to the forgetfulness of Belshazzar and his contemporaries (see 5:22). That was the queen mother.[38] She was evidently from a previous generation, and was not part of the feast, probably because she was considered too old to enjoy that kind of carousing. She heard the rowdy celebrations come to a deathly halt, then the anxiety and confusion. So she came to see what was going on (see 5:10).

38. The Aramaic word is 'queen', which can refer to any female person who has been married to a king. Even in our own times, Queen Elizabeth II's mother, after the death of her husband, King George VI, was always referred to as '*Queen* Elizabeth the Queen Mother' (once a queen, always a queen). Which of the previous Babylonian kings this unnamed woman was married to, or whether she was queen by virtue of being Nabonidus' mother, we cannot say.

Reflection:

When has God been merciful to me, calling me to repent, before I got further into sin or wrongdoing?

What insights into God's revelation have I learned from people or churches that are not part of my denomination or movement?

What steps could I take to actively seek wisdom and understanding?

Chapter 7
Out of Favour
(Daniel 5:10-12)

Cast aside

'Don't be alarmed! Don't look so pale!' the queen mother says to Belshazzar. 'There is a man in your kingdom who has the spirit of the holy gods in him.' She explains how Daniel had served King Nebuchadnezzar and 'was found to have insight and intelligence and wisdom like that of the gods', as well as 'a keen mind and knowledge and understanding, and also the ability to interpret dreams, explain riddles and solve difficult problems. Call for Daniel, and he will tell you what the writing means', she confidently tells him (5:10-12).

At one time Daniel had held the most senior position in King Nebuchadnezzar's court. Now, twenty-three years after his patron's death, not one person out of the 1,000 at the feast had any recollection of him. The queen mother's suggestion was the only positive one being put forward, and Belshazzar was ready to grasp at any straw. 'So Daniel was brought before the king' (5:13). Behind those words, we can well imagine royal officials in a panic, rushing hither and thither, asking frantically if anybody had heard of an old chap called Daniel, or Belteshazzar, and if they had any idea where he might be.

Life can be like that. We can sacrifice so much for our career, working long hours, evenings and weekends, forgoing time that we could have spent with our spouse, our children and our friends, never quite finding much time to be alone with God. Then, once we have left or retired, the organisation to which we devoted so much quickly forgets us. I worked for a large bureaucracy for twenty-five years. I was often told that the day I walked out of the door for the last time, I would be largely forgotten within a week. I knew it was true, because I had seen it happen with so many other people who had left. Indeed, after the first few months of retirement had passed, I have had almost zero contact with anybody in the organisation where I worked.

Often we do not receive even gratitude or acknowledgment for all those extra hours that we put in, all that nervous strain that we put ourselves under, all those sacrifices that we made. The Sydney Opera House is one of the most iconic buildings in the world and is now a UNESCO World Heritage Site. A Danish architect, Jørn Utzon, won the competition for its design, and for seven years its construction dominated his whole life. Then a different New South Wales government was elected which was hostile to his way of working, and he was unceremoniously thrown off the project and replaced. Seven years later, when the building was completed, in 1973, he was not invited to the opening ceremony and his name was not even mentioned – though, like Daniel here, his contribution was ultimately recognised, in his case many years later.

Worse still, like Daniel, we may be at the height of our career and the wind of change in our political environment blows us out of our position. In Europe or America, the government changes colour and the supporters of the old regime are cast aside or relegated to relatively unimportant places. A new US president comes into office and sweeps away all the senior officials and ambassadors of the previous administration, appointing his own nominees who are more to his taste and way of thinking.

Even within the same political party, a change of leader can bring about a radical change of fortune. When Boris Johnson became UK prime minister in 2019, he filled his cabinet with Brexiteers, and many very able MPs who were Remainers were left out in the cold. When Keir Starmer took over the leadership of the Labour Party, he spent the first year or more purging representatives of the hard left from the key positions which they had enjoyed under Jeremy Corbyn's leadership.

A new senior manager comes to a company and they root out or sideline those whom they perceive as having been close to their predecessor. They make their own appointments to positions of power and influence, so that those people will be grateful, loyal and beholden to them. Ability and experience often play no part in this. Daniel stood out for the excellence of his abilities, as the queen mother testifies. But it did not stop him from falling out of favour.

I had a colleague who was very able and had a personal friendship with a very senior manager because she had worked closely with him and was highly valued by him. She had privileged access to this manager; her plans and suggestions invariably found favour; and she was promoted very rapidly. Then her patron retired and his successor seemed to resent anybody who had been close to his predecessor. All of a sudden my colleague found herself on the outside, with the cold winds of suspicion and disapproval blowing round her.

Even in a church, when a new vicar, minister or senior pastor is installed, those who worked closely with the previous leader may not always find it easy to adjust to the new incumbent. They may feel that their contribution is not being valued in the way that it was previously, and they may find that they are no longer included in the inner circle of decision-making.

In fact, ability and experience may even work to our disadvantage when a new regime takes over. We see this in the case of King Rehoboam, who had just come to power in Israel and was faced with a potential rebellion in his kingdom (see 1 Kings 12). He consulted the proven, experienced counsellors of his father, Solomon, and they gave him wise advice, to be a servant to those who were disaffected and to give them a favourable answer; then they would always be his servants. However, he cast them aside, disregarded their experience and ability, and preferred to consult with the young men who had grown up with him. Their impetuous advice, to reject the demands of the rebels out of hand and give them a show of strength, appealed to his vanity. So he followed it – to disastrous effect. His kingdom split into two and he ended up governing only two instead of twelve tribes.

I have met so many people over the years who felt that they had been cast aside in their work or in their church, that they had not been given the responsibilities or status commensurate with their abilities. Some people waste many years nursing resentment and regretting that their talents and gifts have not been recognised, in their job, in their church, among their friends. Others spend years waiting for the change of leadership or attitude that never comes. Still others conclude (erroneously) that God has cast them aside and forgotten them; they fall into despair, and may even turn away from him.

There have been times when I felt cast aside. I recall one situation where I was persistently sidelined when it came to promotion and advancement. My boss even said to me, 'Michael, I have tried my hardest to push your case; but someone, somewhere is blocking everything I try; and I cannot find out who it is.' I never did find out, though I had my suspicions. I did not benefit from the sudden reinstatement that Daniel experienced; but in due course God opened the way for me to move in a promotion to a completely different department.

When I retired and came back to live in England after twenty-five years abroad, I anticipated being involved in various projects in different parts of the world, based on my wide humanitarian aid experience and on certain promises that I had received. Most of those promises never materialised. Doors kept closing in my face, and I became increasingly frustrated. I felt locked out of all the plans that I had anticipated and I lost a sense of purpose for this new phase of my life.

Finally, I made the decision to confront the leaders of one particular organisation as to why they had not fulfilled their promises to me. It was then that I heard the words in my inner self (not audibly), 'It is me who has closed the doors.' They hit me like a shockwave, and I knew that they had come from God. When I had recovered from the shock and picked myself up (or rather, let God pick me up), receiving those words prevented me from becoming bitter or resentful against those whom I felt had let me down and not kept their word. It began a process of accepting my situation and focusing more attention on writing.

We have no record of Daniel's behaviour or attitude during his time out of favour. But, from the way he conducted himself before King Belshazzar, it is clear that he had not turned away from God. He had remained faithful to him, and his relationship with him was as strong as ever. That is the challenge we face in the times when we feel cast aside.

Reflection:

Can I identify an experience when I felt cast aside, perhaps by other people, by an organisation or even by God?

How did I react to this experience? Is there still any residual hurt or resentment over how I was treated? If there is, what steps could I take to resolve matters?

How did that time affect my relationship with God?

How might I be able to use positively my negative experiences of being cast aside?

The wilderness

Being cast aside felt, for me, like being thrust into the wilderness. Daniel sits in a long line of people far more illustrious than me who have had that experience; and it is encouraging to see that they came through it. The rabbi Saul was dramatically converted and was on fire to prove conclusively to the whole Jewish world that Jesus really was their long-awaited Messiah. Yet he spent a number of years in obscurity, in his home city of Tarsus, doing we know not what. Finally Barnabas sought him out – and the text implies that he had to search quite hard to find him – to join the newly flourishing ministry in Antioch (see Acts 11:25-26). Nowhere in the writings of Paul (Saul's new name) is there any trace of resentment or regret over this 'silent period'.

Wang Ming Dao was a prominent Chinese Christian leader who was also cast aside. He spent twenty-five years in a Communist jail, sixteen of them in solitary confinement. He shared these words with a Western visitor:

> When I was put in jail, I was devastated. I was sixty years old, at the peak of my powers. I was a well-known evangelist and wished to hold crusades all over China. I was an author. I wanted to write more books. I was a preacher. I wanted to study my Bible and write more sermons. But instead of serving God in all these ways, I found myself sitting alone in a dark cell. I could not use the time to write more books. They deprived me of pen and paper. I could not study my Bible and produce more sermons. They had taken it away. I had no one even to witness to, as the jailer for years just pushed my meals through a hatch. Everything that had given me meaning as a Christian worker had been taken away from me. And I had nothing to do.[39]

39. Ronald Boyd-Macmillan, *Faith That Endures* (Lancaster: Sovereign World, 2006), p. 307.

That is being cast into the wilderness in the most extreme manner. Yet Wang Ming Dao went on to tell his visitor:

> 'Nothing to do except get to know God. And for twenty years that was the greatest relationship I have ever known. But the cell was the means.' His parting advice was, 'I was pushed into a cell, but you will have to push yourself into one. You have no time to know God. You need to build yourself a cell so you can do for yourself what persecution did for me – simplify your life and know God.'[40]

The enforced lockdowns because of Covid pushed many of us into the kind of cell which Wang Ming Dao speaks of. Such periods of withdrawal, whether voluntary or enforced, are essential for deepening our relationship with God. Just as our lungs breathe in and out in a rhythmic manner, so there are times when we move out into the world around us, followed by times when we withdraw from it to renew our strength. That was how Jesus functioned while he was on earth. As well as his times of demanding public ministry, he frequently made space to be alone to pray or to get away from the crowds and be with his closest disciples (see Matthew 8:18; 14:13; 15:21; 15:39; 17:1-9; Mark 1:35, etc.).

Even before he embarked on his public ministry, directly after being baptised and filled with the Holy Spirit, Jesus was led by the Spirit into the wilderness, where for forty days he was continually tempted by the devil (that is the sense of the Greek verb). Finally, he so vanquished the devil that he left him alone for a time (see Luke 4:1-13). That wilderness experience was a crucial foundation for the three years of ministry which followed. It could not have been avoided.

Jesus refers to this kind of wilderness experience under a different metaphor when he envisages us as branches of the true vine. 'Every

40. Boyd-Macmillan, *Faith That Endures*, p. 308.

branch that bears fruit my Father prunes so that it will be even more fruitful' (John 15:2). We enjoy a season of fruitfulness, then comes a pruning, followed by a season of withdrawal, during which the branches may even look dead.

When we moved to our present house, there were two apple trees in the garden which bore good fruit but had not been pruned for a long time, so they had become misshapen. We called on a tree surgeon to prune them back. He told us that they were already fifty years old; after the pruning they would probably not bear fruit in the subsequent two years, but his pruning would give them twenty-five more years of fruitfulness. Times of pruning are difficult seasons, all the more so when people tell us (with the best of intentions) that we have forfeited the favour of God, or they purport to identify barriers in our relationship with him. However, such times are essential if we are to remain fruitful for the long haul.

As we mentioned, we are told nothing about Daniel's wilderness years in the court of Babylon during the reign of King Belshazzar. We do not know how he survived them, but we do know that when he came back into the public eye, in the presence of the king and all his nobles, he had maintained his faithfulness to God, his sharpness and his gifts; and there was not a hint of personal resentment.

Reflection:

When have I felt cast into the wilderness? What did the wilderness feel like? How did I react to it?

Jesus established firm foundations for his ministry on earth through his forty days in the wilderness. What has been established in my life through my wilderness experiences?

Looking back, when have I felt that I was in a season of pruning? What did it feel like? How did I react to it? What fruit did it bear in the longer term?

Chapter 8
A Man Skilled in His Work
(Daniel 5:13-28)

Serving before kings

The king's messengers eventually find Daniel and bring him to the king (see 5:13). I envisage them discovering him in some back office in the depths of the palace, far away from the king's quarters, carrying out some menial, routine function. Like Joseph many centuries earlier when he was suddenly called to appear before Pharaoh (see Genesis 41:14), he probably needed to be hurriedly washed and brushed and given clothes suitable for a royal audience.

In that back office, Daniel had no doubt had plenty of time to reflect on his former career with Nebuchadnezzar, how he had interpreted the king's dreams, warned him of the consequences of not changing his ways, then seen him fall into insanity, humble himself and be restored by God's grace to being greater than ever before. He must have gone over it time and time again, for he repeats every detail of it to King Belshazzar, omitting nothing of any significance (see 5:18-21).

He would quite probably have often reflected on Proverbs 22:29: 'Do you see someone skilled in their work? They will serve before kings; they will not serve before officials of low rank.' God had certainly fulfilled that word in his life in the past; but had that time come to an end, never to return? His skill had not deserted him, but royal audiences were a thing of the past.

Can that promise in Proverbs be relied on? That was the question which I put to the Lord one day. I was working in an international organisation, tantalisingly close to the corridors of power, but often seemingly excluded from them. His reply took me aback: 'Every week you serve before kings.' 'But how, Lord?' I asked. 'When you stand up each week before the 400 people in your church to serve them, you are standing before 400 kings and queens. To me they are every bit as royal as any earthly king or queen.'

It took me a while to work out what God was saying. Then I remembered that we who trust in Christ are 'a chosen people, a *royal* priesthood' (1 Peter 2:9). Our elder brother, Jesus, is 'KING OF KINGS' (Revelation 19:16), so we have royal status, through adoption; and even royal blood, through being in Christ.

These words changed my attitude to church leadership – which can be very tough at times. It absorbs a lot of effort; a wide range of problems and issues are constantly surfacing; and there are few measurable outcomes. The world may not attach much value, importance or significance to those leading and serving in churches. But the Lord has a completely different value system. 'What society sees and calls monumental, God sees through and calls monstrous' (Luke 16:15, *The Message*).

In fact, it was only after I had retired from my job that the Lord reminded me of how his promise in Proverbs had also been fulfilled literally in my life. While responsible for our organisation's office in Kabul, I had numerous meetings with Ashraf Ghani, who went on to become president of Afghanistan until the Taliban took over. On other occasions I met with António Guterres, Secretary-general of the United Nations, when he was High Commissioner for Refugees. Incidentally, he is one of the most impressive senior political figures I have ever encountered. At a reception he would not just socialise with the people of power, as high-ranking politicians and officials tend to do; but he would make a point of going round the room and speaking to every single individual, however high or low their status.

Then just a few months before I retired, I was called to interpret at a meeting in Chad involving Idriss Déby, the president of that country. It was there that I realised as never before the mortality of those who occupy positions of power. He had then been ruler of Chad for more than twenty years, having had a military background and seized power in a *coup d'état*. Yet he told us, 'I have been a warrior president for my country. But I would like to be remembered as a president who really did good for his people and improved their lives.' Whether he achieved this before his untimely death in an uprising in 2021, history will give its verdict. But this man who held absolute power in his country for more than thirty years wanted most of all to be known as a person who did good for his people.

That is my story of serving before kings. Here is somebody else's story that warmed my heart. Pastor Mick Fleming is a former drug dealer who set up Church on the Street in Burnley, which he describes as 'a faith in action charity that lifts people out of poverty while providing a space for worship.'[41] Among their activities are food support, a daily drop-in, accommodation support, recovery groups, church services, mental health support, medical support, benefits advice, funeral support and a charity shop. Pastor Mick is not the most obvious person who would be chosen to stand before royalty. Yet on 20 January 2022 he and his church received a visit from the Duke and Duchess of Cambridge, and at the end of the visit he was able to pray a blessing over them.

So, there are Daniel's story, my story and Pastor Mick's story. You too will have a story; and yours will, of course, be different – although I do not know how. What we can be sure of, on the authority of Jesus, is that

41. https://www.cots-ministries.co.uk.

'Scripture cannot be set aside' (John 10:35). 'The words of the LORD are flawless, like silver purified in a crucible, like gold refined seven times' (Psalm 12:6). So, we can be confident that, if we are skilled in our work, the promise of Proverbs 22:29 will in some way be fulfilled for us. If you feel that it hasn't, then keep reminding God about it, as I did.

Daniel had been in close contact with many powerful people in Babylon, including King Nebuchadnezzar, its absolute ruler. He too had experienced their mortality behind all the pomp and power of their office. So, when he was suddenly and unexpectedly called upon to stand before King Belshazzar, he was not overawed. He knew that the king was just another human being caught up in the trappings of power. He was therefore able to speak to him with calmness and confidence.

The courtiers who were escorting him would have had a rather different perspective. There was a crisis in the court, feelings were running high, and their positions could be under threat. So they would have been giving him all kinds of advice *en route* to the king. 'You'd better be able to interpret those letters on the wall. You are our last hope.' 'If you can't, I wouldn't want to be in your shoes.' 'Be careful how you speak to the king. He is in a very agitated frame of mind.'

Reflection:

What does being 'skilled in my work' look like for me? Are there things I could do to improve my skill levels? Note: 'my work' is much wider than paid employment; it covers anything which God has called me to do, however big or small.

How have I seen the promise of Proverbs 22:29 fulfilled in my life? If not sure, am I willing to ask God how he has fulfilled it, or intends to fulfil it?

How have I seen the promise of Proverbs 22:29 fulfilled in the life of friends, family members or people in my church?

The big chance!

Once Belshazzar has established Daniel's identity, he begins by flattering him (see 5:13-14). We can discover a lot about how people function by the way in which they relate to us. We often treat people how we ourselves would like to be treated if we were in their position. So, it seems that the king was rather partial to flattery – not unusual for somebody in his position. The king's words also betray a certain embarrassment. Here he was, asking a favour from a man whom he had long ago discarded. His flattery exposes his own lack of judgement and moral bankruptcy. For if Daniel was as outstanding as Belshazzar was claiming, why had he not appointed him to a key position long ago?

The king explains his problem to Daniel and offers him the same magnificent reward as he had offered to his wise men (see 5:15-16). Here is Daniel's big chance! He has languished out of favour for many years. Now at last he has the opportunity to make a name for himself. All he has to do is flatter the king a little and build a relational bridge with him. But he refuses to do so, because his primary concern is to be faithful to God. His first words to the king are astounding: 'You may keep your gifts for yourself and give your rewards to someone else. Nevertheless, I will read the writing for the king and tell him what it means' (5:17). Had an official ever spoken so frankly to a ruler in those times and still survived?

That is only the beginning. Daniel goes on to tell Belshazzar in some detail of how inferior he is to his predecessor Nebuchadnezzar, whom Daniel had served. He reminds him that Nebuchadnezzar, despite his greatness (much greater than yours, he implies), was humbled by God when 'his heart became arrogant and hardened with pride'. He recounts how Nebuchadnezzar ultimately responded by humbling himself and acknowledging the sovereignty of God; and so he was restored (see 5:18-21). Daniel accuses Belshazzar of having the same arrogance as his predecessor. 'But *you* have not humbled yourself, though you knew all this' (5:22-23). Hang on, Daniel! What on earth are you playing at? This is not the way to win friends and influence people!

Daniel knew exactly what he was doing. He was responding faithfully to the prompting of God; and we can identify five factors which influenced him to speak in this way. First of all, he wanted to make clear to the king and the assembled nobles that God's judgement in sending the hand to write on the wall was directly related to their character and behaviour. To those who were accustomed to worshipping idols, this was a novel idea. Their idols were usually fashioned in the light of their own desires and lusts. Idols required regular sacrifices and devotional acts (often sexual); but the suggestion that a god might require certain standards of moral behaviour would have been completely alien to them.

Belshazzar's wickedness had been evident from the beginning of his father Nabonidus' reign, when a coup overthrew and murdered the boy-king Labashi-Marduk after only a few months on the throne. Belshazzar would inevitably have been involved in that bloodshed; and evidently his character had not improved in the seventeen years since then. He and his father had persistently ignored the example set by their illustrious predecessor Nebuchadnezzar (see 5:18-23).

The people at the feast needed to be told that behaviour has consequences. The hand was not, therefore, a random event, not some ghost from the past trying to spoil a good party. God himself had sent it (see 5:24) as a direct result of their arrogance and dishonouring of him.

Secondly, God wanted Daniel to give a clear explanation to all those at the feast why the hand had come at this specific time and why it had written these specific words. Moral standards in Babylon had declined to such an extent that Belshazzar was prepared to 'set himself up against the Lord of heaven', drinking profanely from his holy vessels (5:23). His nobles' glorying over the Lord's supposed weakness in relation to the gods of metal, wood and stone required a response from heaven.

Thirdly, Daniel separated out the Lord's message from his own personal feelings. Like Wang Ming Dao in his Chinese prison cell, Daniel would have been at his most wise, productive and fruitful during his wilderness years. Yet he does not speak in a fit of pique, with seventeen years of rejection, frustration and bile bubbling to the surface and overflowing. He utters not one word of personal complaint at the way in which he has been treated since Nabonidus and Belshazzar took over the kingdom.

Our personal feelings can easily interfere with the message which God wants to give. Many years ago I was asked to read the Old Testament lesson at a service where our bishop was present. It was a passage from Isaiah decrying Israel for their disobedience. Wanting to impress, I read it with all the gusto and passion that I could muster. I sat down and felt quite good about my reading. At the end of the service my minister, who has a wonderful gift of discernment, said to me, 'Mike, there was too much of your own anger in that reading.' It took me aback; but on reflection I knew he was right. Since then I have sought to be more aware of my own emotions when giving any word from God, asking him that they do not unnecessarily distort his message.

Fourthly, Daniel did not allow fear to hold him back from speaking a very unpalatable message to the king (see 5:18-28). Maybe he remembered Proverbs 29:25: 'Fear of man will prove to be a snare, but whoever trusts in the Lord is kept safe.' Fear traps us, renders us immobile, just as a snare traps an animal and immobilises it. Fear holds us back from obeying God and from openly confessing our faith. 'It is with your heart that you believe and are justified, and it is with your mouth that you profess your faith and are saved' (Romans 10:10). Both are equally important.

Daniel did not allow any such fear to control him. He was well aware of the potential danger of imprisonment or execution if he got on the wrong side of the king. But he had received a clear message from God, and he saw no reason to dilute it. He is a wonderful example of these words of a seventeenth-century hymn:

> Fear him, you saints, and you will then
> have nothing else to fear.[42]

You might say, 'It was OK for Daniel; he was old, he was out of favour; so he wasn't risking very much.' Well, the prospect of imprisonment or execution is never pleasant, however old one might be. Pain is still experienced in old age. Daniel's courage here is consistent with his faithfulness to God throughout his life.

Fifthly, Daniel had no desire whatsoever for personal gain. He shunned the idea that 'godliness is a means to financial gain', which the apostle Paul warns against in 1 Timothy 6:5. He believed the word God had given him and therefore he knew that Belshazzar was pretty well finished. He had no interest in the king's rewards and refused to try to ingratiate himself with him. This is so different from the way in which the world around us functions. 'Those who exercise authority … call themselves Benefactors' (Luke 22:25), and people strive and fight to obtain benefits from them.

In the international organisation where I worked, there was no profit motive. So one of the key drivers for the staff was promotion to a higher

42. Nahum Tate (ca. 1652-1715) and Nicholas Brady (1659-1726), 'Through All the Changing Scenes of Life', https://www.jubilate.co.uk/songs/through_all_the_changing_scenes_of_life_jubilate_version.

grade. The annual promotion exercise was always one of the most tense times of the year. Many people shifted into 'me-first' mode, and even longstanding friendships could be damaged by attempts at self-advancement. Many of my colleagues were focused on promotion, on a higher status and salary, on being noticed by those in positions of power.

There is nothing inherently wrong with being promoted or earning more money. The issue is our attitudes and our priorities. Justin Welby, Archbishop of Canterbury, is a wonderful example here. He reached the very top of the Anglican tree, but in his biography he is quoted as saying that he never actively sought any of the roles to which he was promoted because he was always content in the job that he was doing.[43]

Daniel was cast in the same mould. His priority was to be faithful to God and do his job well. If that meant passing on to the king a very unpalatable message, he did not hesitate to do it. Promotion, riches and honour were accepted if they came to him; but he was not actively seeking them. He knew the truth of what the American monk Thomas Merton is reputed to have said many centuries later: 'People may spend their whole lives climbing the ladder of success only to find, once they reach the top, that the ladder is leaning against the wrong wall.'[44]

Reflection:

If I feel that God has given me a word for somebody, how can I prevent my personal feelings and desires from distorting it when I speak it to them?

43. Andrew Atherstone, *Archbishop Justin Welby: The Road to Canterbury* (London: Darton, Longman & Todd, 2013).

44. This is widely attributed to Merton, but there is no hard evidence for him actually having said it. Stephen Covey later on makes a similar quote in his well-known book, *The 7 Habits of Highly Effective People* (New York: The Free Press, 1989).

Is there a situation in the past where I can now recognise that this distortion occurred? What can I learn from it?

How important to me are career advancement, a higher status job and a higher salary? How do these desires tie in with my faithfulness to God?

Do I know a Christian who has a high status or high salary job? Would I be willing to ask them to tell me about their journey to such a job and how they have maintained faithfulness to God in it?

Advance warning

Daniel is totally confident that he will be able to read the writing on the wall for the king and tell him what it means (see 5:17). This suggests that God had already given him the interpretation, or at least key elements of it, before he even came into the room. There are many other examples in the Bible of this kind of prior knowledge.

For example, King Jeroboam sent his wife in disguise to enquire of the prophet Ahijah about their son's illness. 'The LORD had told Ahijah, "Jeroboam's wife is coming to ask you about her son, for he is ill ... When she arrives, she will pretend to be someone else."' Even though he was now blind in his old age, 'when he heard the sound of her footsteps at the door, he said, "Come in, wife of Jeroboam. Why this pretence?"' And he gave her the bad news which the Lord had already revealed to him (1 Kings 14:1-18).

Simeon was 'righteous and devout. ... It had been revealed to him by the Holy Spirit that he would not die before he had seen the Lord's Messiah' (Luke 2:25-26). This prior knowledge of God's purposes prepared him to respond when the Holy Spirit prompted him to go into the temple courts at exactly the same time as Mary and Joseph took the infant Jesus there. He was able to recognise that this child born of very ordinary parents really was the Messiah, even though he did not fit the mould of the saviour whom most Jews were expecting (see Luke 2:27-35).

Prior knowledge of God's purposes enabled Jesus to maintain his focus on the Jewish people (see Matthew 15:24; Romans 15:8). He made sure that all his movements were in line with that. So, when revival broke out in a Samaritan village, he stayed there only two days, then moved on to the Jews in Galilee (see John 4:39-43). His Father had told him that the final act of his life on earth had to be played out in Jerusalem, so he made sure that he was there for the Passover feast at which he would be arrested, tried and executed (see Luke 13:33; 18:31-33).

This gift of prior knowledge and awareness helps us not to deviate from God's purposes. It prepares us in advance for what may happen, as Daniel was prepared here. I experienced it shortly after I went to live abroad. I went with my family on holiday to Switzerland, where we took the opportunity to visit a couple who were good friends and had moved there. Towards the end of our time together the husband said to me, quite out of context with what we were talking about, 'Mike, the Lord has shown me that you are going to have a church in Brussels.'

That is the only word of prophecy I ever heard this man give to anybody, before or since. After we had left them, I said to my wife, 'Well, that was ridiculous. I'm called by God to work in an international organisation, not to lead a church.' Less than a year later our pastor unexpectedly moved back to America and asked me to take over the leadership of the church on a bi-vocational basis. I felt that it was right for me to reply positively to his offer. It was only later, when times were difficult and I began to wonder whether I had done the right thing in taking on church leadership, that this word from my friend came back to me. God had warned me in advance, and that gave me reassurance that I was indeed walking in his purposes.

A possible alternative explanation is that Daniel had no advance knowledge, but took one look at the writing and immediately discerned its meaning. There are people who have an acutely accurate prophetic gift, but this is quite rare. Most of us receive rather vague impressions or words at first. Then as we speak them out, by faith, we find that the impressions and words become clearer and sharper. Daniel had spent a lifetime honing his ability to 'interpret dreams, explain riddles and solve difficult problems' (5:12). So he was able to rapidly understand the meaning of the writing.

Quite probably Daniel's interpretation to the king was a combination of some prior knowledge and some immediate discernment. While he was being led to him, impressions and words would have begun to form in his mind as he listened to God. Then, when he came into the room and saw the writing, these impressions were confirmed and became sharp and clear, so that he was able to speak without hesitation to the king.

As I mentioned in Chapter 6, the letters seemed to refer to units of money, which did not make any sense. Daniel was able to decipher them by recasting the words. Aramaic (like Modern Hebrew) is a language in which only the consonants are written. The vowels are supplied by the reader. It is like reading the phrase, YR DYS R NMBRD. This seems strange to us who are familiar with vowels and consonants, but with practice it becomes automatic.

It does mean, however, that some consonant groups can have different meanings, if different vowels are added to them. Think how many different English words can be formed if vowels are added to the consonants MN (the first two letters of the writing on the wall): man, men, amen, mean, mine, moan, main, mane, moon, omen. Daniel's insight from God was that the vowels were not the obvious ones, and that the apparent nouns were in fact verbs.

Mene was not Mina, a unit of money, but the verb, with the sense of *numbered.*

Tekel was not a shekel, a unit of money, but a verb meaning *weighed.*

Parsin needed to be reduced to its singular form, *Peres*; then it became a verb, meaning *divided.*

Putting the three together, the meaning was then straightforward. Daniel told the king, 'God has *numbered* the days of your reign and brought it to an end. … You have been *weighed* on the scales and found wanting. … Your kingdom is *divided* and given to the Medes and Persians' (5:26-28). The judgement of God had fallen on Belshazzar, and there was no escape.

Reflection:

What experience have I had of God giving me prior knowledge of something? How did that help me?

If nothing comes to mind, is there a friend or family member who has had such an experience and is willing to share what they learned from it?

In order to receive prior knowledge, I need to set aside time to listen quietly to God. When could I set aside such time? It need not be particularly long – quality is more important than quantity, and starting small is easier to maintain.

Chapter 9
Fallen is Babylon the Great! (Daniel 5:29-30)

Presence and reaction

We might have expected a powerful ruler such as Belshazzar to fly into a rage and yell at Daniel, 'I don't want to hear this kind of thing. You're just a bitter old man. Get out of my sight!' – or worse. But the king was badly shaken; and so were his nobles. As Daniel spoke words from God to interpret the writing on the wall, the presence of the Spirit of God flowed through those words and silenced anybody who may have wanted to speak up against him.

It is a precious experience to become aware that the words which you are speaking to somebody are imbued with the Spirit of God, observing the Spirit falling and deeply touching the person. We see it when Stephen was called to explain himself before the Sanhedrin, the Jewish ruling body. 'All who were sitting in the Sanhedrin looked intently at Stephen, and they saw that his face was like the face of an angel' (Acts 6:15).

They listened in silence to Stephen's long speech until they could bear the conviction of his words no longer. Then they 'covered their ears and, yelling at the top of their voices [to drown out the Spirit], they all rushed at him, dragged him out of the city and began to stone him' (Acts 7:57-58). People will not always react positively to the presence of the Spirit, especially those who are tied in to a rigid religious framework.

Thankfully, the pagan Babylonian king and his nobles did not react in this way. They were reduced to silence, but their conviction that what Daniel was saying was true seems only to have been at surface level. For there is no indication of them wanting to change their behaviour in response to the word. In that banqueting hall they experienced what Habakkuk had prophesied many years earlier (in another context): 'Woe to him who says to wood, "Come to life!" Or to lifeless stone, "Wake up!" … The LORD is in his holy temple; let all the earth be silent before him' (Habakkuk 2:19-20).

Silence before God has always been appreciated by some groups of Christians, most notably the desert fathers and the Quakers. Recently it has come much more into the mainstream as a spiritual discipline. It is only in the last few years that I have appreciated its value. Sitting, standing, walking or cycling silently with God has immeasurably deepened my relationship with him. In those times I make no requests to him; I ask him no questions. I simply enjoy being with him, expressing my love and adoration to him and receiving his love. It is one of the most wonderful experiences in the world, all the more so in our society where we are subject to the constant background noise of music, radio, television and smartphones.

Solomon, one of the wisest people who ever lived, knew the value of silence. He gives us good advice about entering into the presence of God, which he expresses under the image of 'going to the house of God': 'Guard your steps when you go to the house of God. Go near to listen. … Do not be quick with your mouth, do not be hasty in your heart to utter anything before God. God is in heaven and you are on earth, so let your words be few' (Ecclesiastes 5:1-2). It is better to actively seek silence with God than to be forced into it as Belshazzar was.

At that Babylonian feast there was another dynamic at play. Like King Herod many centuries later, 'because of his oaths and his dinner guests' (Matthew 14:9), Belshazzar could not afford to lose face. Even though he may not have taken Daniel's words to heart, he had little option but to carry out his promise and reward him. Maybe he also hoped against hope that promoting him to a prominent position might somehow persuade God to change his mind – just as he tried to appease his idols. After all, would God really allow the invasion of a kingdom whose third ruler was somebody 'who has the spirit of the holy gods in him' (5:11)?

Our presence in an organisation, whether for work, leisure or charitable or voluntary activities, will always make a difference. For we take the presence of God, who is living in us, into that situation. The apostle Paul explains it: 'Thanks be to God, who in Christ always leads us in triumphal procession, and through us spreads the fragrance of the knowledge of him everywhere.' However, this fragrance does not guarantee the success of the organisation to which we belong. For, although 'we are the aroma of Christ to God among those who are being saved ... a fragrance from life to life', there is a flip side to the coin: 'among those who are perishing ... we are a fragrance from death to death' (2 Corinthians 2:14-16, ESV).

Your presence in an organisation may actually bring death to it by exposing underlying godlessness and wickedness. The company you work for may go bankrupt or be obliterated in a takeover. The sports team in which you play may be relegated. The country in which you live may suffer a serious economic or political crisis. The empire with a godly third ruler is about to fall to the Medes and Persians.

The presence of only ten righteous people could save a city (see Genesis 18:32). Sadly, there were only four of them in Sodom and Gomorrah – Lot, his wife and their two daughters – and so the cities were destroyed (see Genesis 19). Could Babylon have been saved if there had been only ten righteous people in it? Sadly, it seems that there were not.

The demise of an organisation in which we work or are otherwise involved does not mean that God has abandoned *us*. Far from it! Daniel continued to prosper under the new rulers of Babylon, as we will see in Daniel 6. In every circumstance, 'God's solid foundation stands firm ... with this inscription: "The Lord knows those who are his," and, "Everyone who confesses the name of the Lord must turn away from wickedness"' (2 Timothy 2:19).

Reflection:

What experience have I had of a word from the Lord being given (by myself or by somebody else), which significantly changed the atmosphere of a place? How easy or difficult was it for the person to give the word? What was its ultimate outcome?

How much time do I spend in silence before God? What might hinder me from making this a more significant part of my life?

What difference does my presence make to situations in which I am involved (work, leisure, family, charity ...)? How could I make more of a difference? Are there other Christians in those situations who could join with me in this?

Fulfilment

Having invited the king to keep his gifts and give his rewards to somebody else (see 5:17), Daniel now accepts them (see 5:29). To refuse would have been to shame Belshazzar publicly; and there was nothing to be gained by that. Shaming people rarely brings a positive outcome. The apostle Paul demonstrates this in his dealings with a group who had fallen down in their moral behaviour and were tolerating abusive and disgusting practices – and this was a church! Like Daniel, he avoided shaming them. He did not hold back from strong criticism, but he stressed, 'I am writing this not to shame you but to warn you as my dear children' (1 Corinthians 4:14).

Having received the king's gifts, even Daniel must have been surprised by the immediacy of God's timing, by the speed in which Belshazzar's kingdom was brought to an end. '*That very night* Belshazzar, king of the Babylonians, was slain, and Darius the Mede took over the kingdom, at the age of sixty-two' (5:30-31). Only a matter of hours after Daniel had delivered his warning, Belshazzar was dead and Babylon was in the hands of the Medes and Persians!

What effect did such a dramatic fulfilment have on the hearts and lives of those who experienced it and who managed to survive the invasion? From what we can tell, not a great deal. Not one of the nobles and officials seems to have turned to the Lord. Nobody is recorded as having sought out Daniel to know how to follow the God whose will and power had been demonstrated in such a spectacular way.

Quite the opposite! Only a few months later, driven by jealousy and the desire for power, 'the chief ministers and the satraps[45] tried to find grounds for charges against Daniel in his conduct of government affairs' (6:4). The capacity of human beings to fail to see the hand of God even in the most dramatic of events should not be underestimated. Look at Pharaoh with Moses, how every time there was a new plague, a new manifestation of the Lord's power in his kingdom, he hardened his heart.

'Your word, LORD, is eternal; it stands firm in the heavens' (Psalm 119:89). When Daniel read the handwriting, he brought something eternal and firm into that banqueting hall. He was surrounded by people occupying positions of power – that was a precondition for being

45. We shall meet the word 'satrap' several times in the rest of the book. The term refers to a provincial governor in the empires of ancient times. Nowadays it is used to refer to any subordinate or local ruler, usually with the implication of corruption (presumably because of the habitual behaviour of ancient satraps).

present at the feast. But their power was temporary – much more fleeting than any of them realised. Daniel had very little power in their eyes; he was only a low-ranking court official. Yet it was he who introduced something eternal into that Babylonian court, something which from that moment onwards began to work destruction it. And within a few hours it had brought it down.

That is the power of the prophetic word: it brings something eternal, something from the realm of heaven, something firm and solid into our transitory earthly situation. That is why the household of God is 'built on the foundation of the apostles and *prophets*' (Ephesians 2:20), not on the foundation of the pastors and teachers. The apostles have a foundational, establishing ministry, and the prophets bring the eternal, heavenly dimension into the newly founded church. Without that foundation the effectiveness of pastors and teachers is blunted, unless they themselves also have prophetic gifts. In the worst-case scenario, pastors and teachers end up exercising their ministry without heavenly authority, a trap into which the Jewish teachers of the law had fallen in Jesus' day (see Matthew 7:28-29).

This eternal, heavenly dimension sets the Church apart from all other organisations and draws people to her. The ground for her foundation was prepared by John the Baptist, who himself was a prophet (see Matthew 11:13-14) and was mandated to 'Prepare the way for the Lord' (Matthew 3:3). His speaking the word of the Lord enabled the decrees of heaven to be enacted in the earth. Followers of Jesus are called to continue in that same vein today.

Indeed, we can see this still happening. In July 2019 John Wright, National Director of Vineyard Churches UK and Ireland, interviewed Carol Wimber and Bob and Penny Fulton, three of the pioneers of the Vineyard movement in the 1980s.[46] Towards the end of the interview,

46. https://www.youtube.com/watch?v=97dOO3vlFJc.

Carol shares a prophetic word that she felt was for the global Church. 'It's coming,' she says. 'It's coming soon; it's so big; it's huge; it's wonderful; it's terrible; it's like nothing we've ever seen before. Masses of people will be brought in. God needs everybody in their place in the body of Christ to handle it. Get what God has called you to do, and do it with your whole heart.'

Carol recounts how that word, along with others that she received, prompted her to repent and pray for many people whom she and other Vineyard leaders had taken out of Christian ministry without hope of restoration. This prepared the way for many of those people to spontaneously contact her and be brought back into Christian ministry, to be put back into the places which God had for them in the body of Christ.

When this interview was played at the Vineyard National Leaders Conference in January 2020, I, along with many others, was excited to think that Carol was speaking of some great revival move of the Holy Spirit, bringing masses of people into the kingdom of God. Shortly afterwards, the Covid pandemic broke out, fulfilling everything that she had said, but in a wholly unexpected way – another example of the dangers of interpreting a prophetic word purely with human logic. Carol's word gave direction to the Church on how to prepare for the pandemic; and for how to prepare for coming out of it. 'Surely the Sovereign LORD does nothing without revealing his plan to his servants the prophets' (Amos 3:7).

Jesus acknowledges Daniel as a prophet (see Matthew 24:15) because for many years, under various rulers, he prepared the way for the decrees of God to be enacted in the hostile environment of the Babylonian court. During the reign of Nebuchadnezzar this led to the king's repentance, which is always the Lord's primary aim (see 2 Peter 3:9; Ezekiel 18:23). During Belshazzar's reign it led to judgement. Today the Lord is still placing his people in difficult and hostile situations. He is inviting them to speak into those situations the words that he gives to them, so that they might 'prepare the way for the Lord'.

Reflection:

How do I feel when I am shamed? How do I cope with this?

Can I recall a situation where I (or somebody close to me) shamed another person in order to achieve a desired result? What was the longer-term outcome of this shaming?

Can I recall a situation when God's rapidity in fulfilling his word surprised me? What prompted such rapidity?

When have I seen a prophetic word bring about lasting change in a situation? Are there situations that I am aware of where such a prophetic word is needed? Will I commit myself to praying for that word to be released?

One day that changes the world

Babylon was a place of glory and splendour, the capital of the most powerful empire in the world. As we saw in Chapter 4, Nebuchadnezzar, its most illustrious king, had undertaken a massive building campaign designed to demonstrate to the world its power, magnificence and wealth. It is easy to see why, in the dream which God gave him, the Babylonian Empire is represented as a head of pure gold (see 2:36-38).

Those living alongside Daniel in the royal court at Babylon must have thought that the good times would never end. They were like the turkeys that are fattened up for Christmas. For ninety-nine days they glut themselves on an abundant supply of food. They get fatter and fatter, and say to themselves (if turkeys were capable of reflection!), 'This is a wonderful life. It will surely go on forever.' Then on Day 100: Chop! The turkeys become Christmas dinners, without ever having had the slightest inkling of what was coming.

For many years the inhabitants of Babylon were able to live in wealth and luxury, on the back of the resources and tribute exacted from the many lands which they had conquered. As riches and luxury grew, so decadence set in – as has been the case with so many empires throughout history. The Babylonians hardly noticed the slide; they were so focused on enjoying the good times. Then suddenly, in just One Day, they were taken totally by surprise. '*That very night*' – the night when Daniel foretold the end of the kingdom – 'Belshazzar, king of the Babylonians, was slain, and Darius the Mede took over the kingdom' (5:30-31).

It might be argued that it was rather unfair of God to give Belshazzar only a few hours' notice of the destruction of his empire. However, for decades the Babylonians had had access to the Jewish Scriptures. If they had bothered to pay attention to the word of God within them, they would have found these words of Isaiah (47:5-9):

> Sit in silence, go into darkness,
> queen city of the Babylonians;
> no more will you be called
> queen of kingdoms. …
> Now then, listen, you lover of pleasure,
> lounging in your security
> and saying to yourself,
> 'I am, and there is none besides me.
> I will never be a widow or suffer the loss of children.'
> Both of these will overtake you

in a moment, on a single day:
loss of children and widowhood.

The history books are full of One Days which radically changed the course of history and brought an end to the good times. One Day in October 1914 Archduke Franz Ferdinand, heir to the Austro-Hungarian throne, was assassinated in Sarajevo. This unleashed a chain of events which led to the First World War. The decades of prosperity of the Victorian and Edwardian eras were swallowed up in the costs of war, heralding two decades of unemployment, economic and political turmoil in Europe in the 1920s and 1930s.

One Day in October 1929, after nine years of a continuously rising American stock market, which some economists said could never end, the New York stock market crashed. Over the following three years, stocks lost 89 per cent of their value and did not return to their pre-crash levels for another twenty-five years.

> Thousands of people saw their fortune, or any money they had in the bank, disappear. … Investors lost their money in the Crash and could not pay their debts. Many banks closed, ordinary people lost their savings and people lost all hope for the future. People could no longer buy consumer goods like cars and clothes. As a result, workers were made redundant, other workers' wages were cut and … by the end of 1929, 2.5 million Americans were out of work.[47]

One Day in September 1939 Adolf Hitler ignored Britain's ultimatum and invaded Poland. Britain declared war on Germany. The peace which the First World War was supposed to have created in permanence was

47. https://www.bbc.co.uk/bitesize/guides/zcb4srd/revision/2.

shattered after only twenty-one years. Sixty million people lost their lives in the ensuing six years of the Second World War. Although Britain ended up on the side of the victors, the war left her economy in ruins. Rationing continued for another nine years,[48] and within twenty-five years she had lost her empire.

One Day in September 2001 Arab terrorists commandeered four planes to crash into and destroy strategic buildings in the USA. The post-Cold War global peace was shattered, and its anticipated economic 'peace dividend' vanished. Suddenly the world became a much less safer place. Under the Cold War each side knew who the enemy was and kept a careful eye on them. This new enemy, 'terrorism', cannot be easily defined or identified. Nobody knows quite when, where or how it will next rear its ugly head.

One Day in November 2019, the first Covid-19 case was detected in China – though it took the Chinese government several weeks to report this to the outside world. The ensuing pandemic dealt a massive blow to the global economy. People all over the world faced restrictions on their daily life that they could barely have imagined. Hospitals were brought to breaking point. More than 6 million people died. Fear settled on huge swathes of the population. The world will never be the same again.

It is rather surprising that these 'One Days' catch us unawares, when history is riddled with so many of them. Even a person who is neither philosopher nor economist, and is avowedly agnostic understands this. The controversial footballer, now manager, Joey Barton reflects in his autobiography:

> Empires rise and fall. Kings live and die. ... Generally, when things are going well, people say, 'Happy days. Let's buy, let's borrow, let's

48. I know this from first-hand experience. I was born in 1953, eight years after the end of the war, and in my memory box is the ration book which was issued to me during the first year of my life.

> lend.' Then, suddenly, Armageddon strikes. ... Everyone goes, 'Oh s***!' That's when the clever people emerge. You only realise who hasn't got trunks on when the tide goes out.[49]

Revelation 17 and 18 tell us about another One Day, towards the end of this present age, at a time when there will be a glorious, godless, global economic empire such as the world has never seen. It will be nicknamed 'BABYLON THE GREAT THE MOTHER OF PROSTITUTES AND OF THE ABOMINATIONS OF THE EARTH' (Revelation 17:5) because of the striking resemblance of its underlying characteristics to the Babylonian Empire which Daniel knew. Even though this empire will consider itself invincible, unchallengeable and eternal, Revelation 18:8 tells us: '*In one day* her plagues will overtake her: death, mourning and famine. She will be consumed by fire, for mighty is the Lord God who judges her.'

These One Days will continue throughout history, right up to the final One Day, when 'the sign of the Son of Man' will appear in heaven. 'And then all the peoples of the earth will mourn' (Matthew 24:30). Like all the other One Days since the flood in Noah's time, that final One Day will hit people totally unexpectedly. Jesus tells us, 'In the days before the flood, people were eating and drinking, marrying and giving in marriage, up to the day Noah entered the ark; and they knew nothing about what would happen until the flood came and took them all away. That is how it will be at the coming of the Son of Man' (Matthew 24:38-39).

'But you, brothers and sisters [who are following Jesus], are not in darkness so that this day should surprise you like a thief' (1 Thessalonians 5:4). Jesus has told us how to prepare for that final One Day, and also for all the other One Days before then: 'Stay awake, alert. ... Be vigilant. ... You have no idea when the Son of Man is going to show up' (Matthew 24:42-44, *The Message*).

49. Joey Barton, *No Nonsense* (London: Simon & Schuster UK, 2016), p. 72.

Reflection:

Are there things that I could do now to prepare myself for the One Days that may come in the future?

Hebrews 12:26-27 speaks of God shaking "'not only the earth but also the heavens." … so that what cannot be shaken may remain'. The Covid pandemic has profoundly shaken the earth. What do I see remaining from that shaking, in my own life and in the world around me?

What does it look like not to be in darkness, so that the day of the Lord does not surprise me like a thief? How can I stay awake, be alert, be vigilant?

DANIEL 6
FINISHING WELL

Chapter 10
Overview of Daniel 6

Introduction

In Daniel 6 we come to an all-time Sunday school favourite: Daniel in the lions' den. Over the years children have delighted in how the good guy is falsely accused, but wins out in the end as a result of a miraculous intervention of God; and the bad guys are routed (though the details of their grizzly end are not usually dwelt on with the children!). Adults also enjoy the story of one man overcoming the intrigue of a whole royal court. We love to see the underdog triumphing, to see how 'one man is a majority with God'[50] and how the fame of the God of Daniel is spread throughout the empire of the Medes and Persians through this one man.

The events of this chapter occur only a short time after those of Daniel 5, when Daniel is a very old man, probably in his eighties. Yet so much has changed in that short intermission. The Medes and Persians have deposed Nabonidus and killed his son Belshazzar. They have taken over in Babylon and have imposed their own laws and customs. A new king is on the throne: Darius the Mede.[51]

The Bible is the only historical source which makes any reference to Darius the Mede or to the Medes being involved in the taking of

50. The quote is from Brother Andrew, founder of Open Doors in *Secret Believers: What Happens When Muslims Believe in Christ* (Ada, MI: Revell, 2007).

51. Not to be confused with Darius I (Darius the Great), Darius II or Darius III, Persian kings who ruled over Babylon later on.

Babylon. Therefore, many scholars deny that there ever was a Darius the Mede and reject the biblical account. However, evidence for events which took place two and a half millennia ago is often very sketchy, and there are serious inconsistencies between what different historical sources say about the fall of Babylon.[52]

We should be very cautious about arguing from the silence of history. Had I been writing in 1850, I could have confidently asserted that the story of Belshazzar's feast in Daniel 5 was pure fiction, because there was no reference anywhere in any historical record or artefact to a Babylonian ruler called Belshazzar. Then everything changed in 1854 when the Nabonidus Cylinders (now in the British Museum in London) were discovered in a temple in Ur, and it was found that they contain specific references to Belshazzar, son of Nabonidus. Maybe one day in the future something will be discovered which refers specifically to Darius the Mede.

It seems that Darius ruled under the overall authority of Cyrus – called Cyrus the Great because he had already ruled Persia for more than twenty years and had created the greatest empire the world had ever seen. 'Darius *received* the kingdom' 5:31, ESV – the literal translation), which implies that it was a gift from another ruler. This is confirmed by 9:1, which says that Darius '*was made* ruler over the Babylonian kingdom', i.e. he was made ruler by somebody else.

By the end of Daniel 6 (v. 28), Cyrus has succeeded Darius and is sole ruler of Babylon; so, by then presumably Darius had died. Cyrus himself died less than ten years after capturing Babylon,[53] so Darius' reign could

52. For example, both the Babylonian Chronicles and the Cyrus Cylinder describe Babylon as being taken without a battle, whereas the Greek historians Herodotus and Xenophon report that the city was besieged. The book of Daniel says that Babylon was taken in one night and Belshazzar was killed.

53. Cyrus was born sometime between 600 and 580BC (historians differ on this) and died on 4 December 530BC. Babylon fell in 539BC.

only have been for a fraction of those ten years. Since he was already sixty-two when he became king (see 5:31), it is not surprising if he did not live for very long afterwards, given the much shorter life expectancy in those days. In fact, he is reckoned by some to have lived for only two years after he became ruler of Babylon.

History tends to be written by the victors. So, once the Persians took sole control of the empire, they could airbrush out any involvement of the Medes, and Darius too. Think, for example, of how much British and American history downplays the crucial role of the Russians in defeating Hitler in the Second World War – and that is only eighty years away, not two and a half millennia.

So, in their version of history, the Persians conquered Babylon under Cyrus and he took over the kingship. That version survives in all of the existing historical documents (which presumably used material based on Persian sources), except for the book of Daniel. When there is a difference between the Bible and other sources, scholars demonstrate their bias if they automatically assume that the Bible is the inaccurate source. In so many other instances it has proven to be accurate. Why not here too?

Reflection:

If I read through Daniel 6 from beginning to end and wrote a short story based on the events of this chapter, what title would I give to it? (Something more imaginative than *Daniel in the Lions' Den*!)

What words or phrases in this chapter particularly stand out to me? What is their significance for me?

Looking back on my family history, what past events or circumstances are recorded very differently in the minds of different family members? Why are there such differences? Am I willing to ask God how accurate my perceptions are?

The long haul

As soon as Darius took over in Babylon, he recognised Daniel's abilities and appointed him as one of his 'three chief ministers' (6:2). The psalms promise, 'The righteous will flourish like a palm tree, they will grow like a cedar of Lebanon. … They will still bear fruit in old age, they will stay fresh and green' (Psalm 92:12-14) – an encouragement to all of us who are nearer the end than the beginning of our life; and a counter to cultures where youth and vigour are glorified and old age is rather deprecated. Daniel is a wonderful example of the truth of those words of Psalm 92. Now well into his eighties, and having already served under two empires and seven different kings,[54] his life is still bearing fruit for God.

We have seen in Daniel 4 and 5 how he was able to remain faithful to God while under the rule of Nebuchadnezzar and Belshazzar respectively. Now he is challenged to be faithful under a new ruler, Darius, working under a new system of government. How was Daniel able to maintain his integrity, trustworthiness and faithfulness to God for seventy years? What enabled him to remain faithful for the long haul? As he reached middle and old age in the very comfortable position of a royal civil servant, how did he avoid the lukewarmness and complacency that the Laodicean church fell into when it became rich (see Revelation 3:14-22)?

54. As well as Darius, he served under Nebuchadnezzar, Nabonidus, Belshazzar and the three kings who reigned briefly in the six-year period between the death of Nebuchadnezzar and the accession of Nabonidus, Belshazzar's father.

If you are younger, you might be thinking that it is irrelevant to have to think about this sort of thing at your time of life – just as thinking about pensions seems tiresome when you are in your twenties. However, I have a friend who as a young man rejected advice to set in place a pension plan. Now, in his late sixties, he is still having to work, whether he wants to or not, to generate enough income to live. It is as a young adult that we lay the foundations for our future pension, if we have the opportunity to do so; and, like Daniel, it is as a young adult that we have the opportunity to lay the foundations of character that will enable us to keep going for the long haul. Pensions may fail as a result of periods of unemployment, sickness or low earnings, or of failure of the pension scheme itself. Good character will never fail us.

Three things stand out about Daniel's faith in his old age. Each of them demonstrates the good foundations which he had built into his life over many years. Firstly, he was uncorrupted by the prevailing climate around him. There was plenty of intrigue and corruption in the court of King Darius. His courtiers plotted to get rid of Daniel when they found that 'the king planned to set him over the whole kingdom' (6:3-4). However, when they searched for grounds on which to accuse him, they had to admit, 'We will never find any basis for charges against this man Daniel unless it has something to do with the law of his God' (6:5).

The apostle Paul tells us that we are to 'be blameless and innocent, children of God without blemish in the midst of a crooked and twisted generation, among whom we shine as lights in the world' (Philippians 2:15, ESV). We could view these words as an exhortation to avoid the corruption of the world around us – things such as scheming against other people (as Daniel's colleagues did), indulging in gossip or character assassination, lying when it is convenient for us, or handling money dishonestly.

Keeping away from such things is very important. However, Paul's encouragement is not to avoid the negative, but to display the positive.

The word translated 'lights' occurs in only one other place in the New Testament, in Revelation 21:11, where it describes the new Jerusalem coming down out of heaven: 'It shone with the glory of God, and its *brilliance* was like that of a very precious jewel'. The light that we are called to demonstrate to the world is the same brilliant light that comes directly from heaven. We are to give the world a foretaste of heaven.

In a society where morals are in flux, we Christians often find ourselves identified by our negative attitudes and our refusal to join in with what is going on around us. A caricature of a Christian is the sandwich-board man gloomily proclaiming, 'The end is nigh!' Negativity was not the focus of the preaching of the early Christians. Nor will it attract people to Christ today. We 'hold fast to the word of life' (Philippians 2:16, ESV) – not to the word of death.

Likewise, Daniel was not recognised for his negativity, for his refusal to join in with the Babylonian court intrigue. He 'distinguished himself ... by his exceptional qualities'. His fellow workers 'could find no corruption in him, because he was trustworthy and neither corrupt nor negligent' (6:3-4). That is exactly what Jesus had in mind when he said, 'Let your light shine before others, that they may see your good deeds and glorify your Father in heaven' (Matthew 5:16). Light is positive, and brings warmth and hope.

Secondly, Daniel's heart was untouched by what Jesus calls 'the deceitfulness of wealth'. This deceitfulness chokes the word of life in us, blocks the heavenly light, and makes us unfruitful (Matthew 13:22). Daniel had the opportunity to live a life of considerable luxury in the royal court. He had been surrounded by stupendous wealth for most of his life. A major part of his responsibilities was what we would today call wealth management (6:1-3). Yet none of this distracted him and turned his heart away from the Lord. He knew the truth of Proverbs 23:5, 'Cast but a glance at riches, and they are gone, for they will surely sprout wings and fly off to the sky like an eagle.'

Thirdly, and perhaps most importantly, Daniel kept his relationship with God alive and vital through the practice of spiritual disciplines. Every day he prayed regularly and he gave thanks to God. Even though he was in such a powerful position, he still recognised his need to ask God for help (see 6:10-11). We too are exhorted, 'Pray continually, give thanks in all circumstances; for this is God's will for you in Christ Jesus' (1 Thessalonians 5:17-18). 'Do not be anxious about anything, but in every situation, by prayer and petition, with thanksgiving, present your requests to God' (Philippians 4:6). These spiritual disciplines are vital if (using Jesus' imagery from John 15) we are to maintain our connection with the vine and if the life-giving sap of the Holy Spirit is to flow through us.

Daniel maintained his fervour for God, even in his old age. This certainly does not happen automatically. Indeed, the Bible has many sad examples of people who started well, but then tailed off in their faithfulness to God as they grew older. The kings of the Old Testament seemed particularly vulnerable to this temptation; for power and luxury can easily lull us into complacency and lukewarmness. Jesus' parable of the sower warns that there are 'those who hear, but as they go on their way they are choked by life's worries, riches and pleasures, and they do not mature' (Luke 8:14).

King Solomon started brilliantly, but as he grew old, his many wives turned his heart after other gods and he set up idols, which polluted the kingdom of Judah for hundreds of years (see 1 Kings 11:4-8; 2 Kings 23:13). The boy king Joash introduced many positive religious reforms at the beginning of his reign, but later abandoned the temple of the Lord, worshipped idols and had the priest Zechariah murdered (see 2 Chronicles 24). King Uzziah 'did what was right in the eyes of the LORD', but later in his life, his pride led to his downfall. He was unfaithful to the Lord and, because he tried to usurp the role of a priest, he was inflicted with the socially isolating disease of leprosy for the rest of his life (2 Chronicles 26).

Our faithfulness to God may also be compromised by hardships and difficulties. The parable of the sower warns of those who 'believe for a while, but in the time of testing they fall away' (Luke 8:13). This happened when it became clear that the apostle Paul's trial before the emperor Nero was not going well and that Christians were becoming *persona non grata* in Rome. He laments, 'Everyone in the province of Asia has deserted me, including Phygelus and Hermogenes. ... Demas, because he loved this world, has deserted me. ... At my first defence, no one came to my support, but everyone deserted me' (2 Timothy 1:15; 4:10; 4:16).

We avoid the lukewarmness of the Laodicean church not only by resisting the negative, but by embracing the positive. 'Be enthusiastic to serve the Lord, keeping your passion toward him boiling hot![55] Radiate with the glow of the Holy Spirit and let him fill you with excitement as you serve him' (Romans 12:11, TPT).

We cannot do this solely by our own efforts. Human enthusiasm burns brightly, then dies down. King David knew this. He confesses, 'You, LORD, keep my lamp burning; my God turns my darkness into light' (Psalm 18:28). When the Spirit of God is burning within us, it consumes any darkness, so that 'your whole body ... is full of light' (Luke 11:34).

We no longer offer up the fire of animal sacrifices, as was required from the Jews under the Law of Moses, because Jesus has made the final sacrifice (of himself) on the cross. Instead, we offer the fire of zeal, a burning spirit mixed with the sacrifice of praise, 'the fruit of lips that openly profess his name' (Hebrews 13:15). There are times when we may feel the zeal flagging, that we 'have forsaken the love we had at first' (Revelation 2:4). At such times the tactic of the devil is to push us towards condemnation, resignation and hopelessness. But Jesus has

55. The Greek verb *zeō*, translated 'boiling', is onomatopoetic, expressing the sound of boiling water.

gracious words for us: 'Consider how far you have fallen! Repent and do the things you did at first' (Revelation 2:5). For, as we saw in Chapter 4, repentance is the doorway into the kingdom of God (see Mark 1:15).

Some time ago I went to hear Ken Loach present one of his films and answer questions afterwards. He is a socialist who for more than fifty years has been making (very good) films exposing injustice in British society – starting in 1966 with the TV drama *Cathy Come Home*, which shocked the British public by showing how the British welfare system was failing homeless people.

I saw standing on the stage a man in his seventies (at the time – he is now in his eighties), still burning with the passion to be an agitator against injustice. What an inspiration! If Ken Loach can maintain his ardour for socialism and justice, then surely I can maintain mine for Jesus Christ and justice! Daniel likewise inspires me. He reassures me that, even though we may have a highly responsible job, enjoy plenty of the world's goods, be under a lot of pressure every day, and come up against opposition because of our faith, we can still stay faithful and finish the race well, keeping our passion towards the Lord 'boiling hot' in middle and old age.

Reflection:

However young or old I am (it's never too late!), what foundations am I currently laying in my life?

Can I identify an older or more experienced Christian whom I respect? Could I ask them how they laid foundations in their life when they were younger which have enabled them to be who they are now?

How have they kept their passion towards the Lord 'boiling hot' as they have grown older? Are there things from their life that I can apply in my own to maintain a passionate relationship with God in the medium and long-term?

Chapter 11
Plotted Against
(Daniel 6:1-9)

Ambition

One of the key themes of Daniel 6 is ambition: the ambition of Daniel's colleagues, which was blocked by him being alongside them; and the refusal of Daniel to place personal ambition before devotion to God and faithfulness to the king. Daniel was appointed by Darius as one of the three chief ministers of the kingdom, with 120 satraps reporting to them (see 6:1-2), probably forty to each minister. It was not long before these 120 people decided together that Daniel represented a serious obstacle to their ambitions. So they began plotting to have him removed (see 6:4).

It was not primarily jealousy at Daniel's position and authority that motivated their plotting, for most of the satraps would have had little hope of gaining such a big promotion and stepping into his shoes. It was more likely that Daniel was thwarting their ambitions, not to be promoted, but to make money and gain power and influence. The Bible does not spell this out, but it is a reasonable assumption in the light of their conduct in this chapter and from what we know about royal courts at that time.

Even today, in many countries in the world, a position of public authority is widely seen as an opportunity for personal gain, for oneself and one's family members. One of the most blatant examples in recent times is Mobutu Sese Seko, president of Zaire (now the Democratic Republic of the Congo) between 1965 and 1997.

> Mobutu perfected corruption; the term 'kleptocracy' was coined for the official system of pillage by which he turned the rich Belgian Congo into a beggar state. ... Some estimates put his personal worth at more than $10 billion, while in the 1990s Zaire's per capita income fell below $200 a year, the infant mortality rate soared and public infrastructure in the capital [and throughout the country] disintegrated. Mobutu spent lavishly on monuments and palaces, building himself an African version of Versailles at Gbadolite [his ancestral home], which had an airport runway that could accommodate a Concorde supersonic jet. It was one of 26 mansions he owned.[56]

This would have been the mindset of the satraps in Darius' court – though they would not have had the opportunity to pillage the public purse on the scale that Mobutu did. The eighty satraps who reported to the other two chief ministers would have hatched corrupt schemes to divert money from the royal treasury into their own pockets, and their chief ministers would have taken a cut of the profits in return for turning a blind eye. But the forty who reported to Daniel found to their dismay that he would not tolerate anything which would cause the king to 'suffer loss' (6:2). So, with their plans for illicit gain blocked, they scratched their heads and wondered how they could get rich quickly. There was nothing else for it: Daniel had to go!

In order to get rid of him, these forty who reported to Daniel needed

---

56. https://www.chicagotribune.com/news/ct-xpm-1997-05-18-9705180259-story.html.

the support of the other satraps and chief ministers, so that their plan did not appear to the king as a personal vendetta against Daniel or an uprising against the three chief ministers. Here they found an open door, because the other two chief ministers had begun to realise the delicacy of their position. They were party to all kinds of corrupt schemes, but their fellow-minister Daniel would have nothing to do with such things; and he was becoming increasingly aware of what they were up to. It would only be a matter of time before he had enough evidence to expose them to the king.

The tipping point came when they learned that 'the king planned to set Daniel over the whole kingdom' because he had 'so distinguished himself ... by his exceptional qualities' (6:3). If that happened, there would be a full-on campaign against corruption and fraud, with the king's blessing, and they were all bound to suffer. They could lose their jobs – or even their heads.

'You desire but do not have, so you kill' (James 4:2). The apostle James could have been commenting on this very story! The ministers and satraps desired money and power, and were willing to kill in order to protect their position and advance their money-making schemes. History is littered with similar murderous covetousness. It started right at the beginning of the human race, when Cain killed his brother Abel because he was jealous of his sacrifice having been accepted by God (see Genesis 4:3-8).

Perhaps the most awful manifestation of the deadly nature of selfish ambition is seen in the Jewish leaders of Jesus' day. Their ambition to maintain their privileged position (see John 11:47-50) drove them to 'crucify the Lord of glory' (1 Corinthians 2:8). Even the Roman governor Pontius Pilate, not the most sensitive individual, 'knew it was out of self-interest that they had handed Jesus over to him' (Matthew 27:18).

Jesus astutely identified the Jewish leaders' ambition in a parable he told just before his arrest. He represented them as the tenants of God's vineyard who refused to give the owner the fruit that was due to him, and mistreated the servants who were sent to collect it. When the owner sent his own son to them, 'they said to each other, "This is the heir. Come, let's kill him and take his inheritance." So they took him and threw him out of the vineyard and killed him' (Matthew 21:33-46).

We may sit back and feel satisfied that we would never do anything as awful as that. But even godly people are not exempt from using illicit means to further their ambition. King David was desperate to marry the woman whom he had got pregnant. So he arranged for her husband to be left in an exposed position during a battle so that he would be killed (see 2 Samuel 11-12). And, there are other ways of killing which we might be more ready to countenance in order to advance our own ambitions or desires: killing a person's reputation, killing their emotional health, killing their plans and ideas.

Earlier in his letter, James says, 'If you harbour bitter envy and selfish ambition in your hearts, do not boast about it or deny the truth. Such "wisdom" does not come down from heaven but is earthly, unspiritual, demonic. For where you have envy and selfish ambition, there you find disorder and every evil practice' (James 3:14-16) When we pursue selfish ambition, we open the door to bitter envy and demonic harassment.

The bitter envy of Daniel's colleagues grew and grew, like invasive Japanese knotweed, taking over their thoughts and desires. It pushed them to spend hours, days, weeks scheming how to get rid of Daniel, trying to find a chink in his armour, desperately looking for some ground on which to accuse him (see 6:4). Without them realising it, their selfish ambition had 'given the devil a foothold' (Ephesians 4:27). The devil 'was a murderer from the beginning' (John 8:44); so it is no surprise that, once he had gained this foothold, he planted thoughts of murder into the hearts of Daniel's colleagues. Likewise, if he gains any foothold in our lives, he will have no mercy on us.

Selfish ambition is alive and kicking today. I have observed power struggles, character assassinations, whispering campaigns, harassment and bullying in all kinds of organisations: government administrations, large and small companies, charities, sports clubs, trade associations, churches. When ambition is thwarted, moral restraint may be cast aside. In the court of Darius it gave birth to intrigue, corruption, flattery, deceit and conspiracy to murder. It is no less dangerous today.

Reflection:

Where have I observed somebody driven by ambition who was willing to trample on others to fulfil that ambition? Did they achieve their ambition? How did their pursuit of ambition change them in the short and long-term? What can I learn from the way in which they behaved?

What are my ambitions in life? How much have I discussed these with Jesus?

Who am I willing to ask if they discern envy or selfish ambition in my life? If it is identified, how can I root it out?

Flattery

After weeks, even months, of trying, the chief ministers and satraps finally realised, 'We will never find any basis for charges against this man Daniel unless it has something to do with the law of his God' (6:5). What a remarkable testimony from his enemies! And what an indictment of their wickedness. They wished to kill somebody who was doing his job well and replace him with a person less honest and less trustworthy.

I have a friend who enjoyed a very successful career in business. He attributes much of his success to his superiors and colleagues knowing that he was a Christian and therefore knowing that they could rely upon his integrity and trustworthiness. He was very fortunate. Not all organisations value these qualities. In one place where I worked for many years, integrity and trustworthiness could be a disadvantage, because they would expose the dishonesty and untrustworthiness of certain people in key positions of authority. As a Christian I sometimes found myself sidelined from certain meetings and projects. I was fairly sure why, but did not have hard evidence to prove it. Those things were done secretively, just as these satraps plotted secretively, behind Daniel's back.

Had the ministers and satraps gone to King Darius and asked directly for him to relieve Daniel of his position, on the basis of some phoney accusation, he would have given them short shrift. So, they needed to disguise their intentions. They hit upon a brilliant way of doing this: using flattery. They went as a group to the king and suggested that he 'should issue an edict and enforce the decree that anyone who prays to any god or human being during the next thirty days, except to you, Your Majesty, shall be thrown into the lions' den' (6:6-8).

Had Darius not been quite so blinded by their flattery, he might have wondered why these courtiers were making this unusual request. He might have noticed that Daniel was not among their number. However, they had been around the court long enough to know how to overwhelm a king's reason. Flattery was the tool to use. They knew that Darius' vanity would be attracted by the idea of being set above all other gods in the kingdom for a whole month. And he took the bait. 'King Darius put the decree in writing' (6:9).

Over the years, I have observed people who were unscrupulous, unfaithful and not especially competent gain the confidence of people in positions of authority and power. One of the main tools which they used to conceal their character and (lack of) ability was flattery. Sometimes it was quite subtle; but often, as with Darius here, it was blatant. Why do powerful people, even when they are highly intelligent, fall for this flattery?

Being taken in by flattery is not unavoidable. For example, when the Jewish leaders recruited a prominent lawyer to accuse the apostle Paul to the governor Felix, he tried flattery. 'We have enjoyed a long period of peace under you, and your foresight has brought about reforms in this nation. Everywhere and in every way, most excellent Felix, we acknowledge this with profound gratitude' (Acts 24:2-3). Given the well-known contempt of the Jews for their Roman rulers, this was sheer duplicity. Felix saw right through it and refused their request (see Acts 24:22-23). He certainly had failings, including a willingness to take bribes and to curry favour with the Jews (see Acts 24:26-27); but giving in to flattery was not one of them.

Being in a position of power and authority can be a very lonely place; and loneliness can make us vulnerable to flattery. One particular meeting of the managers of my department at work sticks in my mind. There were half a dozen of us plus the leader of the department. Prior to the meeting, I had heard every person in the room complain bitterly about the leader, except his personal assistant. They were counting the days to his retirement – though when he finally went, they were not so happy with his replacement either! Only one of the people around that table had a positive view of the leader's capabilities, and some of them would gladly have lent a hand to any plot to get rid of him. That is the loneliness of power.

Who could Darius trust as his friends? Who could he rely on? He would have been well aware of the deviousness of his satraps and ministers. Through studying history, he would have known how many monarchs had been assassinated or imprisoned by their own children, their generals or their courtiers, so that they could take over the throne.

In Babylon, only twenty years earlier, no less than three kings had been murdered in a six-year period.

Church leaders may experience the loneliness of leadership too. Among American pastors, 70 per cent do not have someone they consider to be a close friend; 27 per cent report not having anyone to turn to for help in a crisis situation.[57] I suspect that the situation is little different in other countries. Anglican clergy have told me of how they are taught in their ministry training not to make friends with anybody in their congregation because it could compromise their position.

When you are a leader, whether of a country, a department in a company or other organisation, a charity, or a church, making friends is not always easy. If people take an interest in the welfare of you and your family, there is always the nagging doubt that there might be some ulterior motive behind it, that they may be acting in this way in order to gain privileged access to you.

My experience as a leader is that you tend to receive relatively little positive feedback from those you are leading, unless there are specific mechanisms in place, such as 360-degree evaluations. Perhaps people hesitate to approach you because they think you are too busy or too important. Perhaps they consider that you have no need of positive feedback because you are in such an enviable position (so they think). We humans tend to find it much easier to criticise rather than to encourage. What a leader does receive plenty of is complaints and criticism. After all, if there is something wrong, you are the person who is in a position to fix it (single-handedly, in the view of many people).

When a person comes to a leader with something positive or in a positive manner, it is like a breath of fresh air. The apostle Paul tells his friend Philemon, 'Your love has given me great joy and encouragement'

57. https://www.pastoralcareinc.com/statistics/.

(Philemon 7). Elsewhere he prays, 'May the Lord show mercy to the household of Onesiphorus, because he often refreshed me' (2 Timothy 1:16). Despite being one of the most famous leaders in Church history, he needed encouragement and refreshment; and he blesses those who gave it to him.

The borderline between encouragement and flattery is a fine one. Astute people who wish to promote their own agendas will be aware of a leader's need for positive input. If the leader is prone to vanity, as it seems Darius was, they will not hesitate to use open flattery. If they see that the leader is more discerning, they will seek to disguise their flattery as encouragement.

How can we differentiate between encouragement and flattery? For it is rarely possible to discern the depths of a person's heart. We can ask for the gift of discerning of spirits (see 1 Corinthians 12:10). This is often thought of as the capacity to distinguish between good and evil spirits, or between what is of the Holy Spirit and the human spirit. Those are important aspects of the gift; but it has other facets too. It is equally valuable to be able to discern, through the Holy Spirit, what is in a person's spirit. For, 'The Spirit searches all things, even the deep things of God. For who knows a person's thoughts except their own spirit within them?' (1 Corinthians 2:10-11).

I have found that when you are in a position of leadership you can ask God to reveal what is in a person's heart, if that will help you to lead your people well. I recall a man in my church who wished to become a home group leader. I had some intuitive doubts about him, but could not pin them onto anything. While I was driving to his house to speak to him about home group leadership, I prayed that God would reveal what was in his heart. We had a good chat, then at a certain point in the conversation a flow of really horrible words and ideas came out of his mouth, like a volcano belching out lava. I did not interrupt him. Finally he stopped. He looked at me, somewhat embarrassed, as if to say, 'Why did I say all that to you?' I knew why. It was the answer to my prayer; and it prevented me from giving him a position in which he may have hurt and harmed other people.

The Bible gives us useful pointers to separate out flattery from encouragement. David bemoans the morally degraded state of the society around him: 'Everyone lies to their neighbour; they flatter with their lips but harbour deception in their hearts' (Psalm 12:2). Lies and deception are the bedfellows of flattery and their presence will often betray it. That link can be seen in its most gross form when Judas came to betray Jesus and greeted him with a supposedly friendly kiss and flattering words of respect, 'Greetings, Rabbi!' (Matthew 26:49).

When Elihu begins to answer Job's long catalogue of complaints against God, he declares, 'I will show no partiality, nor will I flatter anyone' (Job 32:21). Partiality also reveals the presence of flattery. The flatterer will praise some people beyond what they merit, whilst decrying others, all to feed the leader with opinions that they want them to hear.

This history of Darius and his courtiers shows how receiving flattery can lead us into a very uncomfortable, even perilous position. There is great danger for the flatterers too, as we will see later in this story. Elihu remarks, 'If I were skilled in flattery, my Maker would soon take me away' (Job 32:22). Engaging in flattery distances us from the presence of God and traps us in a snare of lies and deceit. 'Those who flatter their neighbours are spreading nets for their feet' (Proverbs 29:5). With our feet trapped in this way, we are easily taken captive to do the will of the devil (see 2 Timothy 2:26), as were the satraps in Darius' court.

Reflection:

When have I seen flattery operating, either towards myself or somebody else? How did the person being flattered react? How did I feel about this? What was the end result of the flattery?

How would I differentiate between flattery and encouragement?

How does it feel, receiving flattery and receiving encouragement? What is the difference between the two?

Chapter 12
Arrested!
(Daniel 6:10-17)

Attack

With the decree passed, Daniel faced what billions of people have faced throughout the ages, and are still facing today: an attack on the practice of their religion. This is not an exclusively Christian problem. The respected Pew Research Center reports that in 2019, out of the 198 countries in the world, Christians were harassed in 153, Muslims in 145 and Jews in 89. In 29 per cent of the countries of the world – 57 in total – there were high or very high government restrictions on religion.[58]

Christians are by far the largest religious group being persecuted – although accurate figures for global Muslim persecution are difficult to find. 'More than 340 million Christians – one in eight – face high levels of persecution and discrimination because of their faith.'[59]

---

58. https://www.pewresearch.org/fact-tank/2021/09/30/key-findings-about-restrictions-on-religion-around-the-world-in-2019/.
Various organisations use different figures for the number of countries in the world. I have taken the Pew Research Center's figure.

59. https://www.theguardian.com/world/2021/jan/13/christian-persecution-rises-as-people-refused-aid-in-covid-crisis-report.
A good article on global Muslim persecution (by non-Muslims and by other Muslims) can be found on:
https://www.aljazeera.com/opinions/2018/12/22/muslim-cleansing-a-global-pandemic.

Consider the example of India, the world's largest democracy, and a country whose constitution mandates a secular state, prohibits discrimination on religious grounds and whose Article 25 guarantees the right to freedom of religion or belief. Despite this, persecution of Christians and other religions has significantly increased over the past twenty years, so much so that Open Doors, an organisation dedicated to assisting persecuted Christians, assesses it in 2022 as the tenth worst country in the world for Christian persecution.[60]

CSW, the respected organisation advocating for freedom of religion and belief, reports on India:

> Christians experience violations such as false accusations leading up to arbitrary police detention, arrests and prosecution, forced conversion, hate campaigns, assault, death threats, illegal occupation of churches, forced displacement, acts of public humiliation, disruption of religious gatherings, and the looting and destruction of Christian homes, church buildings, and other church owned properties. The United Christian Forum (UCF) recorded 505 violent incidents against Christians in 2021.
>
> On 14 January 2022, Pastor Rakesh Babu and his family were brutally beaten at their home in Chandauli, Uttar Pradesh, by unidentified men armed with wooden logs as they gathered to pray in their parsonage, a tiny room attached to the church where Pastor Babu has served for the last 15 years. A week before, villagers who claimed to be RSS[61] members and had been threatening the pastor, filed a police complaint against him, claiming that he was a Christian missionary who was making large sums of money

60. https://www.opendoorsuk.org/persecution/world-watch-list/.

61. Rashtriya Swayamsevak Sangh: a right-wing Hindu nationalist, paramilitary, volunteer and allegedly militant organisation in India. It was an RSS member who assassinated Mahatma Gandhi in January 1948.

> through the church. Pastor Babu was threatened with jail if he continued to encourage others to join him in prayer. After his attack, the pastor struggled to get local police to properly register his police report.[62]

Sadly, this example could be multiplied thousands of times in a whole range of countries throughout the world. Look at the websites of organisations such as Open Doors, CSW and Release International[63] to see how Christians are being denied basic rights such as meeting and worshipping together, possessing a Bible or other Christian literature, having their children educated, exercising an economic activity. Many Christians the world over are languishing in prison, are tortured, are ostracised by their families and their society, are subjected to violence, are even killed. There is no sign of this pressure letting up. Daniel stands in a long line of people whose lives have been threatened as a result of their faith.

Even in countries where there is no overt persecution, Christians may still feel under attack. In historically Christian Great Britain many Christians feel the need to be ultra-cautious in expressing their faith in the workplace, especially in the public sector. Offering to pray for somebody might be perceived as harassment or proselytism and could lead to disciplinary action. If you are a public figure openly confessing Christian faith based on the Bible, you risk being hounded by the media, as happened with Tim Farron, leader of the Liberal Democrat Party during the 2017 general election campaign.

Glynn Harrison, in his book on 'God, sex & human flourishing', observes:

62. General Briefing: India, 22 March 2022: https://www.csw.org.uk/2022/03/22/report/5613/article.htm.

63. opendoorsuk.org; csw.org.uk; releaseinternational.org.

> Christians who still cling to the old Christian morality understandably feel overwhelmed. As if from nowhere, the home team suddenly feels like the away team. Worse, after witnessing the junking of their moral convictions, they find themselves cast as an immoral minority, a kind of enemy within. Most Christians no longer feel comfortable even admitting to their beliefs in the public square, let alone advocating them.[64]

Faced with an attack on the exercise of one's faith, there are four possible responses:

1. We can attempt to hide our faith – this is the route taken by the 'secret believers' in countries where persecution is most severe; also by followers of the 'insider movement', people with a non-Christian religious background who consider themselves followers of Jesus but continue to identify themselves outwardly with the majority religious community in their society and observe outward ceremonies of that religion. It is also a path taken by many Western Christians in the workplace today (especially men, in my experience).
2. We can flee from the situation of persecution, either with or without the acquiescence of the persecutors – as is happening in the West today, where we are receiving many Christian refugees from majority Muslim countries, such as Syria.
3. We can seek to adapt our faith so as to avoid hitting the attack head-on, for example by accepting some government restrictions or joining in with government-sponsored religious organisations.
4. Or we can carry on regardless of the attack, as Daniel did.

64. Glynn Harrison, *A Better Story* (London: Inter-Varsity Press, 2017), p. xv.

We find all four responses today in countries where Christians are being persecuted. At one extreme are the estimated 300,000 Christians in North Korea who live their faith in almost total secrecy and even avoid praying or reading the Bible in front of their own children, for fear of being denounced to the authorities. At the other end of the scale are the pastors in Colombia who openly preach against the violence, bloodshed and extortion of the armed groups and drug traffickers operating in their areas, and actively seek to share the good news of Jesus Christ with them. Often they pay for this with their lives.

No one response is universally right or universally wrong. At different times in his life the apostle Paul adopted all four strategies. He says 'To the Jews I became like a Jew, to win the Jews. To those under the law I became like one under the law (though I myself am not under the law), so as to win those under the law' (1 Corinthians 9:20). He hid his convictions about Gentile Christians not needing to observe the Law of Moses (for example, when visiting the Jewish Christian leaders in Jerusalem in Acts 21:17-26). That is Strategy 1.

He applied Strategy 2 in Damascus shortly after his conversion. He fled and was lowered in a basket from a window in the wall and so slipped through the hands of King Aretas and his governor (see 2 Corinthians 11:33). At other times he adopted Strategy 3 and took advantage of Roman law, using his rights as a Roman citizen (e.g. Acts 22:25-29). Then, in many of the cities where he preached, he opted for Strategy 4 and confronted persecution head-on, with all the negative consequences which that entailed (see 2 Corinthians 11:23-27).

It is easy to criticise or judge persecuted believers who adopt one or other of these strategies, without knowing the full picture. Even in the same situation of persecution, the difference of response can cause mutual recriminations. In China there can be tension between believers who join the state-sponsored Three-Self Church and those who refuse to be part of that church and open themselves to persecution by worshipping in unregistered churches. The apostle Paul's words to believers in another situation, where they were criticising each other, are pertinent: 'Who are you to judge someone else's servant? To their own master, servants stand or fall. And they will stand, for the Lord is able to make them stand' (Romans 14:4).

Reflection:

Which person or group do I admire for having adopted one of the above four strategies under persecution? Is there some way in which I could follow their example?

In situations where I have felt my faith to be under attack, which of these four strategies have I adopted?

With the benefit of hindsight, how effective do I consider that this strategy (or these strategies) has been? Is there something that I would do differently if faced with the same situation today?

Defence

So serious was this attack on Daniel that he risked losing his life if he continued to practise his faith openly. The way in which he dealt with it gives us pointers as to how to react when we find that our faith is under attack. The threat may be severe, as with Daniel, or more moderate, such as the threat of being mocked or sidelined in our workplace; but the principles are the same. These pointers will also help us to better understand how to pray effectively for our brothers and sisters who are living under persecution, to help them to stand firm in their faith.

First of all, Daniel did not waste time and energy trying to change things that he could not change. He did not go to his fellow ministers and satraps and plead with them, 'Come on guys, this is just not on. What are you hoping to achieve?' He knew that this was a deliberate, calculated attack, and that they intended to see it through to the end. Nor did he go to the king to point out the impact of the decree on him personally and to ask him to change it. He too knew that the laws of the Medes and Persians could not be repealed (see 6:8).

Often, when we find ourselves in a difficult situation, we plead with God to change circumstances that we ourselves cannot change, hoping that he will intervene. Sometimes he does. However, often he has a different agenda, which is to accompany us through pain and difficult circumstances and to change our hearts. He says, 'When you pass through the waters, I will be with you; and when you pass through the rivers, they will not sweep over you. When you walk through the fire, you will not be burned; the flames will not set you ablaze' (Isaiah 43:2). Many of us would have preferred him to say, 'Don't worry. I'll make sure that you don't have to pass through the rivers or walk through the fire.' We so often seek a change in our circumstances, when God is seeking a change in our hearts, so that we can enjoy a closer relationship with him.

Isaiah says of the Lord, 'In all the distress of his people he too was distressed, and the angel of his presence saved them. In his love and mercy he redeemed them; he lifted them up and carried them all the days of old' (Isaiah 63:9). Rather than the Lord changing the circumstances of his people's distress, it became an opportunity for them to experience his love at a deeper level. In the same way Daniel, as an old man, experienced God's love and mercy in a new way in the lions' den.

Secondly, Daniel did not seek revenge or judgement on those who had set the trap for him, nor on the king who had fallen for the flattery of his courtiers. He knew that the Lord had said, 'It is mine to avenge;

I will repay' (Deuteronomy 32:35, quoted in Romans 12:19). To pursue revenge is to steal from God a prerogative that belongs to him. If we do so, we fail to 'leave room for God's wrath' (Romans 12:19). We may ask God to avenge, but this is like asking a judge to pronounce sentence. We have to wait for his timing in issuing the judgement – and God's timing will most likely be different from ours.

Thirdly, there is no sense of Daniel holding any grievance against God. There is no, 'I've served you faithfully in Babylon for these seventy years, God. Why are you letting this happen to me now?' There is nothing wrong with complaining to God. The writers of the psalms utter many bitter complaints to him (see, for example, Psalm 38; 69; 74; 88; 102; 142). Moses complained about the task God had given to him, and God replied with a fresh revelation of himself (see Exodus 5:22 – 6:3). Jeremiah complained bitterly to the Lord and wished he had never been born (see Jeremiah 20:7-18), but the Lord continued to give him new prophetic revelations. Habakkuk complained to the Lord about him not intervening to counter violence and injustice, and God answered him by telling him more of what he was intending to do (see Habakkuk 1 and 2).

However, if we complain to God, there is no guarantee that he will answer our complaint in the way we expect or hope for. Look at the above examples. Look at the experience of Job. For thirty chapters he bitterly expresses all his complaints to God. Then, when God finally speaks, he does not answer a single one of them. Job has the good sense to realise, 'Surely I spoke of things I did not understand, things too wonderful for me to know. … My ears had heard of you but now my eyes have seen you. Therefore I despise myself and repent in dust and ashes' (Job 42:3-6).

A complaint against another person which remains unsatisfied can leave a sour taste in the mouth, especially if we remain convinced of the rightness of our cause. A few years ago, my elderly mother's gas cooker was condemned as unsafe when it was less than three years old. I complained to the retailer who had sold it to her, but they were not interested as the appliance was more than two years old. I did finally obtain reimbursement of the cost of the appliance through a court order, but it left me feeling very negative about buying anything from that shop again.

Likewise, if we have a complaint against God which is not resolved to our satisfaction, like an untreated wound, it can fester and turn into a grievance; and this will inevitably distance us from him. It is good (though not always easy) for us to say, 'Let God be true, and every human being a liar' (Romans 3:4). When Job accepted that God had a much more complete perspective than he did, their relationship was restored and deepened. On the other hand, I know people who have vowed never again to trust God or to have dealings with him because they hold a grievance against him arising from an unsatisfied complaint.

Fourthly, the attack on his faith did not deflect Daniel from the spiritual disciplines which he had established in his life. For many years he had opened the windows of his upstairs room towards Jerusalem and three times a day 'he got down on his knees and prayed' (6:10). These disciplines had served him well for seventy years in Babylon, and he was not about to abandon them.

It is important to establish spiritual disciplines such as regular prayer and Bible reading *before* difficulties come upon us, while we are still on a relatively even keel. People often hit a crisis and then frantically scrabble around trying to find a way to make contact with God. They are like a person who desperately needs to draw money out of their bank account, but when they go to it, they find that they have failed to keep it regularly topped up.

Even if we have well-established spiritual disciplines, in the heat of a crisis they come under pressure and can easily disappear. However, that cuts us off from the help that we need, and it only plunges us deeper into crisis. Daniel did not fall into that trap.

Fifthly, Daniel knew where to ask for help. An appeal to the king or to any other important person was pointless. But the King of heaven was willing to hear and answer his prayer. So, he gave 'thanks to his God, just as he had done before'. When his accusers 'went as a group, they found Daniel praying and asking God for help' (6:10-11).

The psalmist asks, 'I lift up my eyes to the mountains – where does my help come from?' (Psalm 121:1). Those mountains are the biggest things around me. Can they help? Will some army come down from them to save me? Definitely not! 'My help comes from the LORD, the Maker of heaven and earth' (Psalm 121:2). Babylon was a flat plain; there were no mountains to look up to. But we can imagine Daniel praying through this psalm as he reflected on his plight, thinking of the mountains in his home country, and finishing with the comforting words, 'The LORD will keep you from all harm – he will watch over your life; the LORD will watch over your coming and going both now and for evermore' (Psalm 121:7-8). Memorising Scripture can be a massive help to us in times of crisis.

We see these same five principles being followed by the first Jerusalem church. After healing in the name of Jesus Christ a man who had been crippled for forty years, Peter and John are hauled before the Sanhedrin, the Jewish ruling council, and are threatened with severe consequences if they speak any further in the name of Jesus (see Acts 4:1-22). When they report back to their fellow believers, what will be their response to these threats?

Together they pray a remarkable prayer (see Acts 4:23-30). They do not seek any change of circumstances. Rather, they remind themselves that there will always be hostility between rulers and the Lord Jesus, and that he uses that hostility to achieve his own purposes. Their prayer contains no desire for revenge, nor one word of complaint at the way in which they are being treated. They maintain the spiritual discipline of prayer which they have established (see Acts 2:42), and they ask God for help (see Acts 4:25-28).

The help that they ask for is remarkable. 'Now, Lord, consider their threats and enable your servants to speak your word with great boldness. Stretch out your hand to heal and perform signs and wonders through the name of your holy servant Jesus' (Acts 4:29-30). They ask for courage to be able to do more of the very thing that they have been severely warned not to do! They do not request relief from the attacks of the Jewish leaders, but the capacity to remain faithful under them.

No wonder, 'After they prayed, the place where they were meeting was shaken. And they were all filled with the Holy Spirit and spoke the word of God boldly' (Acts 4:31). Theirs is the sort of prayer that God delights to hear and answer. In Daniel's time 'the Spirit had not been given' (John 7:39). So, even though he was not filled with the Holy Spirit in the same way as those disciples were, God enabled him to continue to practise his faith boldly. Like the disciples, this led to a remarkable experience of God's power, which impacted everybody around him.

Reflection:

Are there circumstances in my life which I am asking God to change? Are there different requests that I could make to him in relation to those circumstances? Have I asked him what he wants me to learn through them?

How do I sense God accompanying me through those circumstances? If I am struggling with this, is there somebody who could help me – perhaps somebody who has held onto God through difficult circumstances themselves?

Which of the five principles in this section has spoken most strongly to me? Why is that?

Condemnation

The plan of the ministers and satraps worked like a dream. They had no difficulty in finding Daniel defying the king's decree by openly praying to his God (see 6:11). They immediately rushed off to the king to remind him of his decree and the fact that it could not be changed (see 6:12). Then they dropped their bombshell: 'Daniel, who is one of the exiles from Judah, pays no attention to you, Your Majesty, or to the decree you put in writing. He still prays three times a day' (6:13).

These men had been watching Daniel's habits over a period of time. Still today, we Christians are being observed, often without being aware of it. Many times I have been taken aback when realising how much this is going on. I recall a friend at work telling me how she had been warned by another colleague about my religious fanaticism. 'He belongs to a dangerous sect and has an office full of Bibles,' she was told. I had never spoken to that person about my faith. Nobody had ever remarked on the presence of (only) two Bibles on my desk, nor on my church. But I was being observed – and some observers chose to disseminate a rather distorted version of reality.

The apostle Paul says, 'We apostles have been made a spectacle to the whole universe, to angels as well as to human beings' (1 Corinthians 4:9). As soon as we engage ourselves in the service of Jesus Christ, we become a spectacle, under observation. Some people are genuinely looking to see if what we profess is consistent with our lives – like the person who came up to me after one Sunday service and said, 'I've been watching you for the six months that I have been coming to this church.'

I had no awareness of this. 'And now I know I can trust you.' Then he asked for some assistance in an important matter.

Other people are looking to trip us up, to find evidence to confirm their view that these Christians really are hypocrites and frauds. I recall a person working for me who was unhappy with a decision that I had made. After bitterly complaining, they turned to me and told me that they were surprised that I, a Christian, should be acting like this. I had never ever discussed Christian faith with them, but evidently they had been watching me for some inconsistency between my belief and practice.

This is not a new phenomenon. The apostle Peter tells Christians living only a few decades after Jesus' death and resurrection, 'Always be prepared to give an answer to everyone who asks you to give the reason for the hope that you have. But do this with gentleness and respect, keeping a clear conscience, so that those who speak maliciously against your good behaviour in Christ may be ashamed of their slander' (1 Peter 3:15-16).

Evidently the one person who had not been observing Daniel's religious practices was King Darius. For, when he realised the effect of his decree, 'he was greatly distressed' (6:14). Daniel was his most trustworthy minister and he could ill afford to lose him. He was the person who had predicted that Babylon would be taken over by the Medes and Persians (see 5:28), so he was totally reliable. The king 'was determined to rescue Daniel and made every effort until sunset to save him' (6:14). But he was stuck fast on the rocks of the inflexibility of his own laws, as Daniel's accusers were only too happy to point out (see 6:15). Even the king could not do what he wanted!

I have worked alongside many people in positions of senior management and political power. It has always fascinated me how difficult it is for them to bring about lasting change in their organisation, even when on paper they have the power to do so. They hit problems of cultural resistance – changing an organisation's culture can take many years. They encounter people both within and outside their organisation who are actively working against them, surreptitiously or openly. They come up against the constraints imposed by the regulations and procedures of their own organisation.

The 1980s comedy series *Yes Minister* encapsulates this powerlessness. It follows the career of a newly appointed, not particularly competent, government minister, Jim Hacker. When he arrives in office, he is full of enthusiasm and intends to radically reform his department's policies. But over a period of time, he becomes increasingly frustrated at his inability to bring in any of the changes which he wants and which he had promised to his voters. He has much less power than he had anticipated. Other departments have conflicting interests that have to be taken into account. The prime minister himself has his own agenda.

Worst of all for Hacker, he inherits Sir Humphrey Appleby as his permanent secretary (chief civil servant), whose role on paper is to enable his policies to be enacted, but whose fundamental aim is to maintain the status quo and thwart any seriously innovative schemes that the minister might propose. Even though it inevitably looks somewhat dated, the themes of the programme remain remarkably pertinent for today. The Sir Humphreys are still alive and well, and are doing their best (or worst) to prevent those in power from carrying out their plans.

So, King Darius had to accept the limitations of his power. Having exhausted every avenue, he reluctantly 'gave the order, and they brought Daniel and threw him into the lions' den'. To leave nothing to chance, 'A stone was brought and placed over the mouth of the den, and the king sealed it with his own signet ring and with the rings of his nobles', so that there could be no clandestine attempt to rescue Daniel (6:16-17).

Reflection:

When have I been aware that as a Christian I was being observed? How did this make me feel? How did I react to that awareness?

If I know that I am going to be observed, how can I avoid being really nervous or uptight about not letting Jesus down or creating a bad impression of Christian faith?

If I mess up, or act in a way that is inconsistent with my profession of faith in Christ, how do I deal with this in relation to people around me who are not Christians?

Chapter 13
Release of Power
(Daniel 6:16-23)

Faith in unexpected places

One might have expected an absolute ruler like Darius to think, 'Well, you can't win them all. Daniel has been a good servant to me, and I shall miss him. I did my best to save him, but it just didn't work out. Too bad!' Oh no! The king's last words to Daniel, spoken in the hearing of his courtiers as he was being thrown into the den, were quite astonishing: 'May your God, whom you serve continually, rescue you!' (6:16).

Where did Darius ever get the idea that Daniel's God could rescue him from a pit full of bloodthirsty lions? No idol had ever done such a thing in the whole of history. Yet Darius thinks that it may just be possible. Such an idea could only have come from Daniel himself. Evidently he had shared with the king how different his God was from all the idols of Babylon and Media. Darius had begun to believe this, and he stays up all night thinking about it (see 6:18). In doing so, he nurtures his faith.

We can easily fall into the trap of thinking that faith is present only in the Christian community. We are inclined to forget that all of us at one time 'were separate from Christ, excluded from citizenship in Israel and foreigners to the covenants of the promise' (Ephesians 2:12). In that state of separation we exercised faith to cry out to God for mercy and forgiveness, and he responded with the miracle of new birth (see John 3:3) and new creation (see 2 Corinthians 5:17). As the old hymn says:

The vilest offender who truly believes,

That moment from Jesus a pardon receives.[65]

We may even resent the suggestion that there are people outside the believing community who have more faith than some of us who are inside it. That was how the synagogue congregation in Nazareth felt after hearing Jesus' first public sermon. He highlighted two outstanding Old Testament miracles, both of which flowed from the faith of a person outside of the Jewish community: a widow from Zarephath in Sidon; and Naaman, the commander of the Syrian army. The reaction of the congregation to the suggestion (from their own Scriptures!) that God had favoured these outsiders over and above most Jews at that time was violent. 'They … drove him out of the town, and took him to the brow of the hill on which the town was built, in order to throw him off the cliff' (Luke 4:24-29).

Although he was sent primarily to the Jews (see Matthew 15:24), throughout his time on earth Jesus worked miracles in response to the faith of people outside the Jewish community: a Canaanite woman (see Matthew 15:21-28); a Samaritan leper (see Luke 17:11-19); a heavily demonised Gadarene man (see Mark 5:1-20); a Roman centurion who demonstrated the most remarkable faith that Jesus had encountered on earth (see Luke 7:1-10).

It seems from these and other examples that when faith is present in people outside the believing community, it brings about a significant shift in the heavenly realm. 'The rulers … the authorities … the powers of this dark world', which the apostle Paul speaks about in Ephesians 6:12, are forced to give ground in the face of such faith. This opens up avenues for heavenly power to be manifested on earth. That is what we

65. Fanny Crosby (1820-1915), 'To God Be the Glory', https://www.hymnal.net/en/hymn/h/39.

see happening when Darius exercised his faith, in tandem with Daniel's.

Darius' successor, Cyrus the Great, also came from a pagan, idolatrous background. Yet the Lord calls him 'my shepherd' and 'his anointed' (Isaiah 44:28; 45:1), the latter being the Hebrew word 'Messiah.' Cyrus openly declared his faith in a proclamation which he made throughout his realm: 'The LORD, the God of heaven, has given me all the kingdoms of the earth and he has appointed me to build a temple for him at Jerusalem in Judah' (Ezra 1:2). He recognised that his rule of all the kingdoms around him was not ultimately due to his political or military astuteness, but to the God of heaven. It was a gift from his hand. Cyrus' faith broke the power of the demonic forces which had held the Jews in exile for seventy years, and enabled the re-establishment of a believing community in Judah. It was Cyrus' faith that kick-started the Lord's preordained purpose.

Where is faith being expressed today in unexpected places? We may well need to search, precisely because those places are unexpected. The faith may be in embryonic form. It may not be burning very strongly. It may even be in danger of being extinguished. Encouragingly, Isaiah prophesies of Jesus, 'a smouldering wick he will not snuff out' (Isaiah 42:3).

A number of years ago I was attending a training session and at the beginning each participant had to introduce themselves and say what they were engaged in. The minister of one of the churches in the city told us, 'I am here to fan into flame the dying embers of faith wherever I find them.' What a marvellous vision! Discovering dying embers in unexpected places! Fanning them into flame!

Where are those dying embers in our communities today? Where is that faith that could so easily go out if it is not nurtured? Could it be that we are often searching too narrowly? Could it be today in the Muslim community, where Jesus is revealing himself through dreams, through friends, through their reading of the Quran (which has a lot of positive things to say about Jesus)?[66] Could it be that he finds a faith and reverence among them which is sometimes lacking even in Christian communities?

Reflection:

Where have I found faith in unexpected places? How could I nurture and encourage such faith?

Where do I see dying embers of faith? How could I cooperate with God in fanning them into flame?

Deliverance

Darius put his faith into action. He fasted and refused any of the entertainments which would normally have helped him to sleep. 'At the first light of dawn, the king got up and hurried to the lions' den. When he came near the den, he called to Daniel in an anguished voice, "Daniel, servant of the living God, has your God, whom you serve continually, been able to rescue you from the lions?"' (6:19-20). Monarchs never hurry anywhere, even today. Has anybody seen a picture of Queen Elizabeth rushing anywhere? Hurrying is what servants and courtiers do. But Darius hurries to the tomb, his courtiers struggling to keep up with him, wondering what on earth he was up to.

Darius' faith overcame any concerns about his image. He would have looked very foolish indeed, had he set aside his royal dignity to run to a tomb and cry out to a dead man. And it was not good for a king to look

66. A very good record of this worldwide phenomenon is Jerry Trousdale's *Miraculous Movements* (Nashville, TN: Thomas Nelson, 2012). It avoids sensationalism and concentrates on well-researched incidents.

foolish! Many of his courtiers would have been involved in the plot to have Daniel killed, and you can imagine them sniggering behind their hands as Darius shouted to Daniel. There was the same reaction from the mourners who had come to bewail the death of Jairus' daughter. They laughed at Jesus when he told them she was not dead, only sleeping (see Mark 5:40). Unbelief and cynicism mocks faith. But, as with those mourners, the courtiers' sniggering soon turned to consternation when they witnessed Daniel's deliverance.

Deliverance is a major theme throughout the Bible: the deliverance of Joseph from prison; the deliverance of the Israelites from slavery in Egypt; the deliverance of King Hezekiah and Judah from the Assyrians; the deliverance of Jeremiah from those who wanted to put him to death – these are just a few, chosen randomly. Greatest of all is the deliverance of Jesus from death, which then led to the deliverance of his people from slavery to sin and from death.

In fact, there are some marked similarities between Daniel's condemnation and deliverance and Jesus' crucifixion and resurrection. So, this history of Daniel can be viewed as a prefiguring of the earth-shattering events in Jerusalem which would take place more than 500 years later: a kind of aperitif, preparing God's people for what was to come. It is as if God was saying to the Jews through this history, 'Prepare yourselves for a Jew who one day is going to be unjustly condemned but will then be miraculously delivered. When that happens you will know that he, like Daniel, is genuine.'

Both Daniel and Jesus are condemned unjustly; both are subjected to a brutal punishment, but God miraculously delivers them both from it. Both of them are sought at first light of dawn by people sympathetic to them: Darius seeks Daniel, and women who had followed Jesus seek him in the garden where he was buried (see Matthew 28:1-10). Both Darius and the women find the man they are looking for alive; both are overjoyed; and in both cases this ushers in a period when the knowledge of the true God is spread about as never before.

Intriguingly, the pagan Darius demonstrated more faith than the women at the garden tomb, even though they had spent three years in Jesus' company and had repeatedly heard him predict his resurrection. They went to the tomb with the aim of anointing a dead body (see Luke 24:1); but Darius was expecting (or half-expecting?) to find Daniel alive. He calls out to him 'in an anguished voice' (6:20), still feeling distressed at having been tricked into signing his death warrant. He was still not 100 per cent sure whether he could trust his gut feeling that there was a God who was capable of rescuing Daniel. But he hung on to the measure of faith that he had. It may have been no bigger than a mustard seed, but it moved a mountain in that lions' den (see Matthew 17:20), if you will pardon the mixed metaphor.

In the garden, when Mary meets the risen Christ, at first she is not able to see him for who he is. Then she hears him call her name, 'Mary'; and she knows that all is well (John 20:16). Likewise, King Darius at first is not able to see Daniel in the half-light of dawn. Then he hears his voice calling out his name, 'May the king live for ever!' (6:21); and he knows that all is well.

Daniel explains to the king, 'My God sent his angel, and he shut the mouths of the lions. They have not hurt me, because I was found innocent in his sight. Nor have I ever done any wrong before you, Your Majesty' (6:22). Once again, a stupendous miracle is totally downplayed (as was the rescue of the three young men from the fiery furnace in Daniel 3).

Daniel could have given us a whole raft of detail on how the angel appeared in the den, what he looked like, how there was a blinding flash of light, how the lions cowered at the sight of the angel, how the angel went round each one individually, shutting their mouths and claws as if with glue, how they prowled around all night in frustration. The king would have listened with rapt attention; and we too would love to have been given more details. However, all Daniel says, in a matter-of-fact way, is, 'My God sent his angel, and he shut the mouths of the lions.'

We see the same understatement with Jesus' miracles during his time on earth. He set the pattern in the very first miracle recorded in the Gospel of Mark (1:23-26). He delivers a man in the synagogue from an unclean spirit simply by doing no more than commanding it, 'Be quiet! Come out of him!' God is a God of power and might, but not of razzmatazz. The Son of God tells us, 'I am gentle and humble in heart' (Matthew 11:29); so, he is not given to ostentation or show. Like Father, like Son.

I suspect this may be one reason why we see relatively few miracles in the West today. We would make too much fuss of them. Newspaper reporters and television crews would be pursuing us as soon as they got wind of them – not to mention the furore on social media. Like the crowds who pursued Jesus from place to place, seeing miracles would become more important than following Jesus (see John 4:48). Maybe this is why some of the most spectacular miracles today are being done in out-of-the-way places, away from the glare of the media.

The king was overjoyed. Not only was Daniel safe, but he now knew that Daniel's God was real and powerful, and could be trusted. 'When Daniel was lifted from the den, no wound was found on him, because he had trusted in his God' (6:23). He had remained faithful to him. It was exactly the same with the three young men when they came out of the furnace. Their onlookers 'saw that the fire had not harmed their bodies, nor was a hair of their heads singed; their robes where not scorched, and there was no smell of fire on them' (3:27). When God intervenes, he does not do things in half measures.

The psalmist encourages us, 'If you say, "The Lord is my refuge," and you make the Most High your dwelling, no harm will overtake you, no disaster will come near your tent. For he will command his angels concerning you to guard you in all your ways' (Psalm 91:9-11). That angelic protection is as available for us today as it was for Daniel then. We do not need to ask angels to protect us. We make the Lord our refuge and the Most High our dwelling, and then *he* commands the protection – just as he did for Daniel in that lions' den.

Reflection:

'Without faith it is impossible to please God' (Hebrews 11:6). Where am I exercising faith, or being challenged to exercise faith, at the moment?

How can I sustain and nurture that faith?

When have I seen somebody miraculously delivered from a harmful situation (it does not have to be as dramatic as the lions' den!)? How was God glorified through that deliverance?

Can I recall a situation where I was unjustly treated, but ultimately vindicated by God? How did I react to the vindication? What difference did it make to my situation?

CHAPTER 14
HAPPILY EVER AFTER?
(DANIEL 6:24-27)

Times of persecution and suffering can release the power of God in a new way. At the time when the New Testament was being written, the apostle Paul and his fellow workers were under so much pressure in the province of Asia (present-day western Turkey) that, he confesses, 'We despaired of life itself. Indeed, we felt we had received the sentence of death' (2 Corinthians 1:8-9). Yet that hardship released the power of God so extensively that, during his two years in Ephesus (the capital of the province), 'all the Jews and Greeks who lived in the province of Asia heard the word of the Lord, and God did extraordinary miracles through Paul' (Acts 19:10-11).

As Daniel came out of the lions' den, the power of God broke through at a new level: to Daniel himself, to King Darius and his subjects, and even to Daniel's accusers. Each of them was impacted, though they did not all live 'happily ever after' as the characters do in the fairy tales. Let us look at each group.

Judgement

1. *The malicious accusers of Daniel* witnessed the power of God, but their hardness of heart meant that it had no effect on them. It was the same with the Pharisees, who saw Jesus cast demons out of people as nobody

had ever done before. But they hardened their hearts and scoffed, 'It is only by Beelzebul, the prince of demons, that this fellow drives out demons' (Matthew 12:24). It was the same on the Day of Pentecost. When the Spirit of God was poured out as never before, some of those present, even though they heard the sound of the violent wind which accompanied the tongues of fire, mocked the believers, saying, 'They have had too much wine' (Acts 2:13).

It seems that this is an age-old phenomenon. In the book of Exodus, more than 3,000 years ago, Pharaoh witnessed God's power in an unprecedented way as plague after plague was inflicted on his country. But after each plague he 'hardened his heart' (Exodus 7:22, 8:15,19,32, 9:7,34), and this brought great harm upon him and his people. So, we are warned, 'Today, if you hear his voice, do not harden your hearts' (Hebrews 3:15). If we do, we risk bringing harm on ourselves, just as Daniel's accusers brought destruction on themselves.

'At the king's command, the men who had falsely accused Daniel were brought in and thrown into the lions' den, along with their wives and children. And before they reached the floor of the den, the lions overpowered them and crushed all their bones' (6:24). There must have been quite a few lions in that den! The fact that Darius was capable of ordering such a brutal punishment, yet could feel such compassion for Daniel, shows the strength of his feeling for him.

The fate of Daniel's accusers graphically illustrates the warning of Proverbs 26:24-27: 'Enemies disguise themselves with their lips, but in their hearts they harbour deceit. ... Their malice may be concealed by deception, but their wickedness will be exposed in the assembly. Whoever digs a pit will fall into it; if someone rolls a stone, it will roll back on them.' The accusers had disguised their malice towards Daniel through deception and flattering words; but their wickedness was publicly exposed. The lions' den, the pit which they had, as it were, dug for Daniel, became their place of destruction.

God's judgement does not always come as quickly and obviously as it did to Daniel's accusers. He deals with those who oppose his people in his way and in his time. There have been severe persecutors of Christians, such as Joseph Stalin in the USSR or Kim Il-Sung in North Korea, who died in their old age of natural causes. '"It is mine to avenge; I will repay," says the Lord.' That same passage warns us, 'Do not repay anyone evil for evil' and 'Do not be overcome by evil, but overcome evil with good' (Romans 12:17-21). Waiting for God to avenge can be very challenging and can really test our faith. What we are asking for may never happen in our own lifetime. But waiting is a necessary discipline, letting God do things in his way – which is invariably better than ours.

I have already mentioned 2 Peter 3:9 several times in this book, but it is such a crucial verse in understanding God's timing in judgement that it is worth repeating: 'The Lord ... is patient with you, not wanting anyone to perish, but everyone to come to repentance.' While Daniel was in Babylon, Ezekiel was giving a similar word to the Jewish community living there: 'Do I take any pleasure in the death of the wicked? declares the Sovereign LORD. Rather, am I not pleased when they turn from their ways and live?' (Ezekiel 18:23).

We see God's heart in the history of King Nebuchadnezzar. In Daniel 3, he tried in vain to kill the innocent Shadrach, Meshach and Abednego; but he was allowed to live and later came to repentance (Daniel 4). Likewise, King Darius' foolishness in signing the decree was forgiven and he was given the opportunity to proclaim the greatness of God throughout his domain. It does not always happen that way – King Belshazzar never repented (see Daniel 5) – but God and all his angels are delighted when it does happen (see Luke 15:10).

Many times I have seen God's judgement fall on people who were opposing or harming Christians, in line with those verses from Proverbs 26. When it happens, the book of Proverbs offers us sound advice: 'Do not gloat when your enemy falls; when they stumble, do not let your heart rejoice, or the LORD will see and disapprove and turn his wrath away from them' (Proverbs 24:17-18).

Daniel followed this advice. He did not ask for his accusers to be punished, nor did he gloat over their destruction. In the same way, it is not helpful for us to vent our anger and frustration by immediately asking for the demise of people who oppose us. When James and John asked Jesus, 'Do you want us to call fire down from heaven to destroy' a Samaritan village which had refused to receive them, he 'turned and rebuked them' (Luke 9:54-55). When the Lord invited Solomon to ask for anything that he desired, he was very pleased that he did not ask for the death of his enemies (see 1 Kings 3:11-12).

If we take matters into our own hands and attempt to call down trouble or harm on other people, we risk placing ourselves on the devil's ground – and he is far more effective than us at using evil and harm. Jesus has taught us 'the most excellent way' (1 Corinthians 12:31): 'Love your enemies and pray for those who persecute you, that you may be children of your Father in heaven' (Matthew 5:44-45). If we follow this and 'bless those who persecute' us (Romans 12:14), we place ourselves out of the devil's reach, because blessing and wishing good for people is incomprehensible to him.

Reflection:

How do I recognise if I am hardening my heart? How can I avoid this? Would it help to talk with a friend about this?

When have I observed the downfall of people who were opposing me, another Christian or a group of Christians? How did I react to this? How do I feel now about how I reacted?

Breakthrough

2. King Darius. The king had seen the power of God openly displayed, and his first instinct was to tell everybody about it. He reminds me of a Belgian friend who was the wife of an ambassador, and so had a wide range of contacts. She gave her life to Jesus Christ relatively late in her life through watching the recording of a Billy Graham crusade. Having made that momentous decision, she went through her (extensive) address book and wrote to every single person in the book to tell them what had happened to her (those were the days before texts and WhatsApp).

Darius had an even more extensive range of contacts, and he was not afraid to take advantage of them. Something very special had happened and he wanted everybody to know. He 'wrote to all the nations and peoples of every language in all the earth' (6:25).

The final words which Jesus spoke to his disciples before he ascended into heaven were these: 'You will receive power when the Holy Spirit comes on you; and *you will be my witnesses*' (Acts 1:8). In other words, you will tell people what you have seen and heard and what the Lord has done for you. I wonder if we Christians have often been too focused on announcing doctrine to the world: You are sinners; Christ died for your sins; you need to turn to him and repent.

Those truths are vitally important; but have I neglected simply telling my story of what I have seen and heard and what Jesus has done for me? 'It is with your heart that you believe and are justified, and it is with your mouth that you profess your faith [i.e. tell your story of what Jesus has done for you] and are saved' (Romans 10:10). Doctrine can be disputed and contradicted; our story cannot – although that does not mean that people will always respond favourably to it – see the apostle Paul's experience in Acts 22, 24 and 26.

It seems that the power of God is often demonstrated to enable testimony to be given to people who have never heard about the living God. In Mark 5, we read of a man who also experienced the power of God at first-hand. He was freed from a legion of demons (around 5,000!), and immediately 'began to tell in the Decapolis [his own country] how much Jesus had done for him' (Mark 5:20).

Most of the people in the Decapolis – a group of ten predominantly Greek-speaking cities to the east of the river Jordan – had never heard of Jesus and would have been surprised when the man freed from the demons started talking about him. He was breaking up unploughed ground. Likewise, most of the 'peoples of every language in all the earth' would have been astonished to find King Darius telling them, 'In every part of my kingdom people must fear and reverence the God of Daniel' (6:26). Most of them would probably never have heard of Daniel, let alone his God.

King Darius goes on to explain why people should reverence the God of Daniel: 'He is the living God and he endures for ever; his kingdom will not be destroyed, his dominion will never end' (6:26). The remarkable insight which this statement shows can only have come from God – just as Jesus told Peter when he showed similar depth of insight: 'This was not revealed to you by flesh and blood, but by my Father in heaven' (Matthew 16:17). In Darius' day, nations chose the gods they worshipped, and they became a symbol of national identity. You did not worship somebody else's gods! Yet Darius confidently declares, 'Here is a God who is actually living – in contrast to our idols – and he has a kingdom that is not limited to any one nation. That's why I am telling you about him.'

Darius sees that God extends an invitation not just to one nation, but to people 'in every part of my kingdom'. Most of the Jews – even their leaders – right up to the time of Jesus failed to see this; but this pagan king did. The Jews mistakenly thought that because God had chosen

Israel as his special people, his purposes were limited to that nation. Exclusivity is a common failing of religious groups; and Christians are not exempt from it.

'His kingdom will not be destroyed, his dominion will never end', says Darius. He had just taken over the Babylon Empire, which had once seemed invincible; and he knew very well that all the empires before that had also come to an end. The past might of the great Assyrian Empire was nowhere to be seen. Probably his empire would also end one day – though hopefully not in his lifetime. Yet he recognises, here is a kingdom that is completely different, one that will not be subject to the same decay and destruction as the earthly empire of which he was ruler. The living God carries on living forever. So, his kingdom does as well. This contrast between the kingdom of God and earthly empires is strikingly similar to the picture in King Nebuchadnezzar's dream in Daniel 2.

Darius goes further: 'He rescues and he saves; he performs signs and wonders in the heavens and on the earth. He has rescued Daniel from the power of the lions' (6:27). The king had seen God rescue Daniel from the power of the lions with his own eyes. But here the king speaks of him performing 'signs and wonders in the heavens'. Such things could not have been deduced from Daniel's rescue. Evidently he had been listening carefully to Daniel telling him about his God – and perhaps about the prophetic visions which he was receiving, some of which are reproduced in the second half of the book of Daniel.

It seems that a spirit of prophecy comes upon the king. For he echoes the words of the prophet Joel, which Peter quotes on the day of Pentecost: 'I will show wonders in the heavens and on the earth, blood and fire and billows of smoke. The sun will be turned to darkness and the moon to blood' (Joel 2:30-31). We should not be surprised to find prophetic words uttered in unexpected places. We should not reject them purely because we have doubts about the person speaking them. Even wicked

Caiaphas prophesied accurately about Jesus, without knowing it (see John 11:49-52).

Reflection:

Who am I telling how much Jesus has done for me? How could I develop strategies to tell more people?

In which nations of the world do I see Christianity significantly growing today? How can I pray for those nations and cooperate with God in what he is doing in them?

What signs of exclusivity do I see in myself or in the Christian community to which I belong? What can I do to counter any that I identify?

Indifference

3. The subjects of King Darius. When a ruler has a dramatic experience of God, it can have an effect on the whole nation that they rule. In our individualistic Western societies we find this hard to understand. When Queen Elizabeth II extolled the virtues of the Christian religion in her annual Christmas broadcast, people may have said, 'That's very commendable' or, 'How inspiring!' or, 'That's her opinion,' or even, 'She should keep her religion to herself.' But I suspect that few listeners changed their belief system as a result of her words.

Yet for most of history it has been very different. For example, the emperor Constantine's conversion in AD312 radically changed the religious situation in the Roman Empire; and Christianity has been the dominant religion in most of that area since then. When Vladimir the Great converted to Christianity and was baptised in AD988, he had his nobles and all the residents of Kiev baptised, and this is taken as the beginning of more than a millennium of Christianity in the Russian lands. Until the Middle Ages, when a ruler converted to Christianity, all of his people converted with him (at least outwardly), as a sign of their loyalty and submission to him.

The final words of Jesus to his disciples have been obscured in many English translations. In the original Greek they read, literally, 'Therefore, having gone, *disciple all the nations*, baptising them, etc.' (Matthew 28:19). Individualism is helpful in emphasising that relationship with God comes through responding personally to him, and not automatically through performance of a religious ceremony or membership of a particular family or group. However, it also has a negative side.

After American atomic bombs were dropped on Hiroshima and Nagasaki in August 1945, Japan unconditionally surrendered to the Allies, and they occupied the country under the authority of an American general, Douglas MacArthur. Shortly after MacArthur's death in 1964, the American evangelist Billy Graham revealed that he had told him that Emperor Hirohito had privately declared his willingness to make Christianity the state religion of Japan. MacArthur, a Baptist Christian, turned down the offer, saying that no nation must be compelled to conform to any religion; choice of religion was an individual, personal decision. The emperor then asked America to send 10,000 Christian missionaries to Japan. Only a handful ever went.[67]

Japan had never before experienced such a shameful defeat. The emperor was ready for his nation to take on the religion of the conquerors. But the opportunity was lost, through the individualistic mindset of General MacArthur and through the failure to send missionaries. The global religious map could have been very different today.

67. https://www.nytimes.com/1964/04/07/archives/general-told-of-barring-offer-to-create-a-christian-japan.html.

Daniel did not waste *his* opportunity. Although we are not explicitly told so, he must have been involved in some way in the decree which King Darius issued, with his name featuring so prominently in it. At the very least he would have encouraged the king to do what his heart was suggesting to him. Quite probably the idea for the decree came from Daniel himself – remembering King Nebuchadnezzar's similar letter 'To the nations and peoples of every language, who live in the earth' (4:1).

The king's decree did not result in the whole of the Persian Empire beginning to follow the Lord, the God of Israel. Its principal religion continued to be Zoroastrianism. However, we can be confident that the impact of the decree was far from negligible. Imperial decrees were not to be ignored! People who had never even heard of the Jews now became aware that their king was ordering reverence to be given to this God who, he claimed, was different, more powerful, more long-lasting than any of the idols that they were worshipping.

At the very least, some people would have wanted to know a little more about this God. 'The message about the kingdom' (Matthew 13:19) was sown into the hearts of those who read the decree, and it found various types of soil there. Much of the ground would have been unfruitful, but there is always somebody who receives the seed and bears fruit – as Jesus explains in the parable of the sower (see Matthew 13:1-23).

The Lord says, 'As the rain and the snow come down from heaven, and do not return to it without watering the earth and making it bud and flourish, so that it yields seed for the sower and bread for the eater, so is my word that goes out from my mouth: it will not return to me empty, but will accomplish what I desire and achieve the purpose for which I sent it' (Isaiah 55:10-11). Exactly what the Lord's purposes were in the words that Darius spoke in his decree, we cannot know. But, based on Isaiah's word, we can be sure that there were purposes and that they were achieved.

What was the long-term effect of the decree? We will not know until the books are opened at the end of the age. Was it this decree that sowed in the mind of Darius' successor, Cyrus, the idea that the Lord was asking him to encourage the Jews to return to Jerusalem and to finance the rebuilding of their temple (Ezra 1:1-4)?

Many centuries later Magi came from the east and followed a star which led them to Jesus' birthplace. When they found him, 'they bowed down and worshipped him … and presented him with gifts of gold, frankincense and myrrh' (Mathew 2:11) – unusual behaviour for such illustrious people towards a seemingly very ordinary Jewish baby. Persia is to the east of Israel. So I wonder if one of the factors which prompted their quest was knowledge of the decree of Darius, passed down through many generations?

Thirty years after this baby's birth, the outpouring of the Holy Spirit on Jesus' disciples was witnessed, among others, by 'Parthians, Medes and Elamites' (Acts 2:9), all of whom came from the area at the centre of the Persian Empire. I wonder what influence Darius' decree had on maintaining in those areas the continuing presence of a community of people seeking the living God?

Reflection:

Where can I see the conversion to Christianity of a ruler having made a difference to the religious landscape of their country? Which rulers am I praying for?

Jesus asks his followers to 'disciple all the nations'. How can I put this into action in my own life? Which nations are on my heart?

Where in my own country can I see an event which has had a long-term positive spiritual effect on the nation? What can I do to encourage it to have even more effect?

The crown

4) Daniel too was impacted in a new way by this display of the power of God. He had narrowly escaped Nebuchadnezzar's death sentence in Daniel 2; but he had never before in all his long life stared death in the face quite so closely as he did in that lions' den. He came out of it with a new confidence, a confidence which enabled him a few years later to receive revelation at a level deeper than ever before ('in the third year of Cyrus', Daniel 10-12).

Daniel would have wholeheartedly agreed with the apostle Paul, who himself 'fought wild beasts in Ephesus' (1 Corinthians 15:32) – maybe literally, maybe metaphorically. Paul testifies that God 'has delivered us from such a deadly peril, and he will deliver us again. On him we have set our hope that he will continue to deliver us' (2 Corinthians 1:10).

At one of the lowest points of my life, in very difficult circumstances, I was finding peace of heart and mind to be so elusive. Then, during a time of prayer, God impressed this scripture on my mind: 'The eternal God is your refuge, and underneath are the everlasting arms' (Deuteronomy 33:27). Through this word I was able to sense – not physically, but somewhere deep in my spirit – those everlasting arms holding me up. I knew instinctively that they would prevent me from falling into the depths of an abyss which seemed to have opened up beneath me. Having felt the protection of those everlasting arms at my lowest point, and having come out to the other side, I have gained a confidence that, whatever adverse circumstances I may have to pass through in future, God's everlasting arms will always be underneath me, preventing me from falling uncontrollably.

I experienced the truth of God's promise which I referred to in Chapter 12: 'When you pass through the waters, I will be with you; and when you pass through the rivers, they will not sweep over you. When you walk through the fire, you will not be burned; the flames will not set you ablaze' (Isaiah 43:2). I felt as if I had nearly drowned in the waves of criticism that had swept over me. I felt as if fire had been licking at my feet, ready to consume me. Yet here I was on the other side of it – permanently changed (for the better, I hope), but not permanently harmed. No doubt Daniel felt much the same way after being preserved in the lions' den.

Not only was Daniel's confidence in God boosted, but his position in the royal court was made firm for the rest of his life. 'Daniel prospered during the reign of Darius and the reign of Cyrus the Persian' (6:28). He had had his share of trials and tribulations, culminating in the lions' den. Some are recorded in the Bible; there were, no doubt, many others that are not. Yet there came a point when God said, 'Enough!' to his trouble and suffering and allowed him to enjoy peace and prosperity.

Suffering is an inevitable part of life in this fallen world. It is neither to be sought nor avoided. The apostle Paul could say, 'I delight in weaknesses, in insults, in hardships, in persecutions, in difficulties' (2 Corinthians 12:10). Yet that same apostle urges us to pray 'for kings and all those in authority, that we may live peaceful and quiet lives in all godliness and holiness' (1 Timothy 2:2).

Some believers are allowed to enjoy peaceful and quiet lives into old age – like Abraham, the father of all the faithful; like Job, after the trials recorded in his book; and like Daniel here. For others, death in old age comes violently: like the apostle Paul, executed in Rome by the emperor Nero; like Polycarp, Bishop of Smyrna, burnt at the stake in AD155 at the age of eighty-six; like Bishop Latimer, burnt at the stake in Broad Street, Oxford by Queen Mary at the age of sixty-eight. None of us can know how it will turn out for us. These things are in God's hands. What we can be sure of is that all of us who have followed Jesus Christ, however we have died, 'will receive a rich welcome into the eternal kingdom of our Lord and Saviour Jesus Christ' (2 Peter 1:11).

The last dated reference to Daniel that we have is in the third year of King Cyrus (see 10:1-4), that is 535BC. He has been mourning and fasting for three weeks and is with a group of men on the banks of the river Tigris. There he receives a vision and important revelation from God. So, he was still practising his spiritual disciplines, remaining faithful to God, right up to his death. Six cities claim his tomb. The most famous one is a centre of pilgrimage in Susa, 400 miles (650km) east of Babylon, in the south of present-day Iran.

In Chapter 13, we looked at the parallels between the lives of Jesus and Daniel. Just as there was a time when Daniel's suffering came to an end so, on the cross, immediately before he died, our Lord Jesus cried out, 'It is finished' (John 19:30). 'After he had provided purification for sins [with all the suffering that this entailed], he sat down at the right hand of the Majesty in heaven' (Hebrews 1:3), where he remains to this day.

While still on earth Jesus told his disciples that he was going to his Father's house to 'prepare a place for them' (John 14:2). He knew that their journey to that house would not be easy. For he told them, 'In this world you will have trouble. But take heart! I have overcome the world' (John 16:33). Our journey to the Father's house may be rather peaceful, or it may pass through suffering or a violent death. However, we will all arrive there if we hold fast to our faith. For Jesus promises, 'I will come back and take you to be with me that you also may be where I am' (John 14:3).

Had Daniel known these words of the apostle Paul, he would have been able to echo them at the end of his long and fruitful life: 'I have fought the good fight, I have finished the race, I have kept the faith. Now there is in store for me the crown of righteousness, which the Lord, the righteous Judge, will award to me on that day – and not only to me, but also to all who have longed for his appearing' (2 Timothy 4:7-8).

The examples of Daniel and Paul, and so many others in the Bible, are such an inspiration to me. They stayed faithful to the end. And so can I too, with God's help. God give us grace to finish our race well, whatever life may bring. May we 'Be always on the watch', praying that we 'may be able to stand before the Son of Man' (Luke 21:36) and so receive from our Lord Jesus the crown of righteousness that is in store for us.

Reflection:

What occasions in my life can I identify when the power of God significantly impacted me? What was the long-term effect?

Whose examples of faithfulness to the very end inspire me? What can I do now to begin to emulate them?

What am I doing now to prepare myself to finish well?

Appendix A
A Suggestion as to How You Might Use This Book

Based on my own experience of studying the Bible devotionally, I would like to offer this suggestion as to how you might read this book in order to get the most out of it. It is only a suggestion, and you may well find a way that is more helpful for you. So please feel free to ignore it.

- Since God has inspired the writing of the Bible, it is good to begin by asking him to reveal himself to us as we read it. A prayer and a short time of silence can be really helpful, dialling us down from whatever we have been doing and helping us to focus on him.
- Then read the relevant Bible passage, followed by the section relating to it, together with other Bible passages that are referenced in the section. Read the Bible in whatever version you find most helpful – or maybe in more than one version, to compare and contrast them. Most of the time I quote from the New International Version; sometimes I have used other versions or made my own literal translation.
- While doing this, be alert to whatever God may be wanting to highlight. It is good to have pen and paper – or PC or tablet – at hand to write these things down. The act of writing or typing reinforces the words. You don't have to be absolutely convinced that it is God who is speaking to you. Just write down what you think or feel, and you can examine and review it at a later date.
- Then reflect on the questions at the end of the section. Some you may find particularly pertinent to you, others less so. Focus on those which you find helpful.

- It is beneficial to draw times of devotional Bible study to a close with an expression of gratitude to God for giving us the Bible and for communicating with us. This could take the form of a prayer, a worship song, a time of silent adoration, or whatever.
- Finally, it is good to close with a short time of silence before entering back into everyday life.

Appendix B
Key Dates Relating to Daniel 4-6

Some of these dates are disputed by scholars. I have taken the ones which are consistent with the biblical record or seem to have most overall support.

640	Josiah becomes king of Judah at the age of eight (2 Chronicles 34:1)
633	Josiah begins to institute religious reforms in Judah (2 Chronicles 34:3)
625-618	Daniel is born some time in this period
609	The Assyrian Empire finally falls, to an alliance of Babylonians and Medes
609	King Josiah dies in battle against the Egyptians
	His son Jehoahaz succeeds him as king (2 Kings 23:29-32)
608	Pharaoh deposes Jehoahaz after three months and installs his brother Jehoiakim as king (2 Kings 23:33-35)
605	Nebuchadnezzar becomes king of Babylon at the age of twenty-five
	Babylon defeats Egypt and Assyria at the battle of Carchemish, and so becomes the leading superpower of the Middle East
	Nebuchadnezzar invades Judah (2 Kings 24:1)
	… and deports Daniel and many other prominent Jews to Babylon (1:1-6)
	King Jehoiakim switches his allegiance to Babylon
601	… then switches his allegiance back to Egypt (2 Kings 24:1)
598	The Babylonians capture Jerusalem
	King Jehoiakim dies, having been attacked and bound

	by the Babylonians (2 Chronicles 36:6), and is buried ignominiously outside Jerusalem (Jeremiah 22:18-19)
597	His son Jehoiachin is deposed by the Babylonians, after reigning for just three months and ten days
	The Babylonians deport all but the poorest people of the land
	… and install Jehoiakim's brother Zedekiah as king (2 Kings 24:8-17)
588	King Zedekiah rebels against Babylon, causing the Babylonians to lay siege to Jerusalem (2 Kings 24:20; 25:1)
587	After an eighteen-month siege, Jerusalem falls and is destroyed by the Babylonians (2 Kings 25)
562	Death of King Nebuchadnezzar
562-556	Three Babylonian kings reign in quick succession: Awel-Marduk, Neriglissar and Labashi-Marduk
556	Nabonidus takes over as king of Babylon, but is absent from the city for long periods of time and leaves its rule in the hands of his son Belshazzar (Daniel 5)
539	Babylon is conquered by the Medes and Persians (5:30-31). Darius the Mede becomes ruler of Babylon, under the authority of Cyrus, king of Persia
	Daniel passes into the service of the conquerors
537	The Jews begin to return to Jerusalem, following a decree of Cyrus, king of Persia (Ezra 1)
	King Darius dies. Cyrus (called 'the Great') becomes sole ruler of Babylon
535	The last dated reference we have to Daniel, 'In the third year of Cyrus', 'on the bank of the great river, the Tigris' (10:1-4)
530	King Cyrus the Great dies and is succeeded by his son Cambyses

Appendix C
The Date of Daniel 4

When did the events of Daniel 4 take place? I put forward the following analysis for your consideration. If you disagree, you may well be more learned than me in ancient history. Any difference should not divide us. And my conclusions do not materially affect the rest of the book.

The Babylonian Chronicles exist only for the first eleven years of King Nebuchadnezzar's reign, up to 595BC, so they cannot help us. On the assumption that the 'seven times' in this chapter represent seven years (see footnote 22), and that Nebuchadnezzar reigned for several years after he recovered his sanity, we are looking for a period of at least ten years.

Ezekiel 29 and 30 prophesies that Nebuchadnezzar 'and his army – the most ruthless of nations – will be brought in to destroy the land. They will draw their swords against Egypt and fill the land with the slain' (30:11). This prophecy was given 'in the twenty-seventh year, in the first month' (29:17).

'The ninth year, in the tenth month' of Ezekiel's prophecies is the 'very date that the king of Babylon laid siege to Jerusalem' (Ezekiel 24:1-2), that is, at the beginning of 588BC. Based on this date, the prophecies of chapters 29 and 30 were given in 571BC. So, at that time Nebuchadnezzar had not yet invaded Egypt. The Jewish historian Josephus places the Egyptian invasion a little after 582BC, but his dates are not always accurate. Ezekiel's dating is consistent with a fragmentary inscription that places the invasion in 568BC, just three years after his prophecy.

Six years after this invasion, Nebuchadnezzar died, in 562BC.

Therefore the ten-year period which we are looking for must end before 571BC, since Ezekiel is unlikely to have prophesied Nebuchadnezzar's military success when he was absent from the throne. We know from the Babylonian Chronicles that have been discovered that Nebuchadnezzar was on his throne from 605BC to 595BC, and we know that he was involved in the fall of Jerusalem in 587BC. Therefore, his insanity could not have begun before 585BC since, after destroying Jerusalem, he would have to return to Babylon and be given a year's warning through Daniel.

Therefore, it seems that this seven-year period of insanity began sometime between 585 and 581BC, a period for which the historical record other than the Bible is largely silent. By then Daniel would have been well established in Babylon, having been there for somewhere between twenty and twenty-five years.